calls us to a deeper, richer, and fuller immersion and investment in friendship. This is a marvelous book.

—Robert Allan Hill, dean of Marsh Chapel, professor of New Testament and pastoral theology, and chaplain to the university, Boston University

This is a beautiful and generous book. Rich in storytelling, rooted in Scripture, drawing on Catholic social teachings and personal experience, Cooper guides us through a treasure trove of resources for building deep connections with others. Cooper makes the case that cultivating friendships is not only essential to human flourishing, but also a deeply faithful way of being Catholic. Profoundly relevant in this time of heightened polarization, this is a resource for all of us who want to connect across lines of division. In defiance of forces that would separate us, Cooper's book is a timely counterargument for embracing the transformative power of unlikely friendships.

—Jennifer Howe Peace, interim University Chaplain, Tufts University (2018–2020), and associate professor of interfaith studies, Andover Newton Theological School (2008–2018)

If beauty will save the world, friendship will hold it together. Cooper offers spiritual resources and stories to inspire a generation to see friendship as the aim of our relationships with those from beyond our traditions, cultures, and practices. For any interfaith organization or clergy group, college campus, or local community seeking to connect across religious differences, *Embracing Our Time* provides a spiritual grounding to sustain the work of tending to these sacred relationships.

—Patrick B. Reyes, dean, Auburn Theological Seminary

Praise for *Embracing Our Time*

Pope Francis, addressing young people in Singapore in fall 2024 said, "All religions are paths to God. I will use an analogy: they are like different languages that express the divine." Lynn Cooper's book is important for Catholics in the parishes and seminaries. We have so many divisions, and with the rise of racism and Christian nationalism, this work is even more needed. Her gentle insights, suggestions, and years of experience can help midwife Catholics to appreciate the richness of living in a pluralistic society, forming interfaith relationships and meaningful collaboration. Parishes, through the Baptismal call of the Laity, can learn from Cooper's experience and theology, as she facilitates students in uncovering the tools at their disposal for interfaith living and justice, especially through the lens of Catholic Social Teaching and praxis. Though challenging, there is also celebration and joy in the doing. We are called to build bridges of friendship and mutual respect for the dignity of all human beings.

—Sister Marie Thérèse (Tess) Browne, SCN, racial justice, interfaith, and labor organizer; recipient of the Bishop James Augustine Healy Award; and Boston Labor Guild Fr. Edward Boyle Award

Lynn Cooper's book on interfaith friendship is a warm embrace of story, theology, and practicality. Every page nourishes the reader and encourages the adventure of interfaith engagement so needed in our time. Be bold! Engage in this journey that can help nourish healing, understanding, and some new growth.

—Sister Simone Campbell, SSS, recipient of the Presidential Medal of Freedom

Lynn Cooper is a wonderful storyteller, as she draws on her many interfaith experiences to show us vividly how interreligious values come to the fore in ordinary life amid the work we do and, above all, in the evolving friendships gifted to us and cultivated over the years. This is a fine book about friendship in interreligious dialogue, but it is more—a rich testimony to Cooper's own life journey, a path enriched by stories of finding God amid the relationships that keep giving vitality to her life and ministry.

—Francis X. Clooney, SJ, Parkman Professor of Divinity, Harvard University

In *Embracing Our Time*, Lynn Cooper brings Vatican II's vision of dialogue to life for our nascent synodal moment, inviting us to view interfaith friendship as a path toward deeper communion. With insights and stories drawn from her work with young people in campus ministry, Cooper vividly illustrates how empathy, deep listening, and friendship can transform both our spiritual lives and the church itself. Her work is a timely guide for communities seeking to embrace Vatican II's call to an open, relational faith.

—Colleen Dulle, associate editor, *America* magazine

Lynn Cooper's book invites Catholics into the enriching world of interfaith friendship, showing how Catholic theology, spirituality, and practice provide a foundation for—not a contradiction to— cross-religious engagement. Her anecdotes are compelling, her reflections thoughtful, and her expertise practical. Cooper offers readers not only new information but also an opportunity to cultivate the necessary disposition for interfaith work, one which she herself embodies and models beautifully.

—Jordan Denari Duffner, author of *Finding Jesus among Muslims: How Loving Islam Makes Me a Better Catholic* and *Islamophobia: What Christians Should Know (and Do) about Anti-Muslim Discrimination*

Lynn Cooper's fine work on friendship is a gift and blessing for the church, for the academy, and especially for readers who come with a personal longing and appreciation for friendship. Jesus said, "I have called you friends" (Jn 15:15). In that very spirit, Lynn Cooper

Embracing Our Time

EMBRACING OUR TIME

The Sacrament of Interfaith Friendship

Lynn A. Cooper

FORTRESS PRESS
MINNEAPOLIS

EMBRACING OUR TIME
The Sacrament of Interfaith Friendship

Copyright © 2025 Fortress Press. All rights reserved. Except for brief quotations in critical articles or reviews, no part of this book may be reproduced in any manner without prior written permission from the publisher. Email copyright@fortresspress.com or write to Permissions, Fortress Press, PO Box 1209, Minneapolis, MN 55440-1209.

New Revised Standard Version Bible, copyright © 1989 National Council of the Churches of Christ in the United States of America. Used with permission. All rights reserved worldwide.

Library of Congress Cataloging-in-Publication Data

Names: Cooper, Lynn A., author.
Title: Embracing our time : the sacrament of interfaith friendship / Lynn A. Cooper.
Description: Minneapolis : Fortress Press, 2025. | Includes bibliographical references and index.
Identifiers: LCCN 2024040717 (print) | LCCN 2024040718 (ebook) | ISBN 9781506499253 (print) | ISBN 9781506499260 (ebook)
Subjects: LCSH: Friendship--Religious aspects--Catholic Church. | Catholic Church--Relations. | Christian Union.
Classification: LCC BV4647.F7 C667 2025 (print) | LCC BV4647.F7 (ebook) | DDC 241/.6762--dc23/eng/20241228
LC record available at https://lccn.loc.gov/2024040717
LC ebook record available at https://lccn.loc.gov/2024040718

Cover image: Yellow-billed magpie, Stellers jay, Ultramarine jay and Clark's crow. John James Audubon, 1785-1851. Sourced from Boston Public Library/Unsplash

Cover design: Kristin Miller

Print ISBN: 978-1-5064-9925-3
eBook ISBN: 978-1-5064-9926-0

Contents

	Acknowledgments	vii
	Introduction	1
1.	Friendship in the Tradition	11
2.	Interdependence and Difference	45
3.	Listening to God, Ourselves, and One Another	69
4.	Sacramental Consciousness and Participation	95
5.	Humility, Courage, and Allyship	125
6.	Wellspring of Hope: The Sacrament of Interfaith Friendship	151
	Notes	173
	Bibliography	181
	Further Reading	189
	Index	191

Acknowledgments

The roots of this book go deep, embedded within relationships that span time, space, and tradition. I am full of gratitude and awe when I reflect on all who have helped bring this work into being.

First off, a big thank you to Ryan Hemmer and Fortress Press for believing in this project from the beginning and for insisting that I begin *here* with these stories and theology. Thank you to Adam Bursi and the entire team at Fortress for bringing me over the finish line and making this book the best it could be.

I am beyond grateful to Drs. Jenny Peace, Celene Ibrahim, Stephanie Edwards, and Eileen Daily. These women have shepherded me through the process, answering phone calls and texts with abundant practical wisdom and joy.

To Rev. Elyse Nelson Winger, whose generosity, support, and encouragement made the writing of this book possible. To our beloved students who are constantly challenging me to grow in new directions and who have blessed me with their stories and questions. To colleagues and friends through the ages: Naila Baloch, Shareda Hosein, Rev. Dr. David O'Leary, Rabbi Jeff Summit, Linda Karpowich, Lauren Bloom, Rev. Dr. Greg McGonigle, Rev. Pat Kepler, Rev. Kerrie Harthan, Venerable Priya Sraman, Walker Bristol, Alex Chiu, Shelby Carpenter, Zach Cole, Lindsey Chu, Venerable Vineetha Mahayaye, Rabbi Jordan Braunig, Abdul-Malik Merchant, Dr. Preeta Banerjee, Rabbi Naftali Brauer, Dr. Ji Hyang Padma, Anthony Cruz Pantojas, Rev. Dan Bell.

ACKNOWLEDGMENTS

To everyone who read early, gnarly versions of chapters. I'm looking at you, Susie Hayward, Meg Berkowtiz, and Nora Bond. I'm grateful for your time, attention, and critical feedback.

To my soul friends: Heather Angell and Chris Davies. You are the DNA of this book.

To my wonderful parents, all the Coopers, Brooks, and Kenneys (Irish Catholic family, y'all). For bringing me into this world and helping me come back to life when I needed it most. You cannot know how much I love you. Thank you for always believing in me.

To R, my best teacher. I feel no closer to the divine than when I laugh with you.

And most of all, to my dear Andrew. You, who inspire me every day and whose casual, loving nudge to make this book "my pulpit" has been a guiding light.

To each of you and so many more, thank you.

Introduction

I have long known that I am called to the in-betweens, the intersections, the liminal space. As a child, I relished the energy in our full house and often felt spirited away by streams of possibility, joining my brothers and their friends to play pond hockey or cheering endlessly at my sisters' all-day swim meets. I was the youngest, happy to be along for the ride, to be in motion, and to witness to the world around me. Sometimes, it felt like I was living in the seams of our family, as if I were resting in the nest of a patchwork hammock, the fabric supporting my weight, its edges stretched around me. I was held close but always found hidey-holes and new places to poke through. I loved it there. It was all I knew, but it was exciting in that in-between place—there was always so much to take in.

As a family, we went to Mass every Sunday—living ritual within ritual. We would pile into the station wagon in the church parking lot and bump into those same families at the Village Market ten minutes later. There, in the back aisle, a special table was set up for just those mornings, mountains of fresh bagels that had made the trip from Brooklyn in the wee hours. In high school, I periodically attended liturgy by myself at the parish the next town over. I relished the safety and comfort of anonymity, being an insider and outsider simultaneously. It was a welcomed relief to take up prayerful space in a new and intentional way—something I was too bashful to do at our home parish. Those experiences of feeling at once known and unknown, seen and unseen, would shape my spiritual life as a young person hungry for meaning and connection. I was on a journey. I was a seeker. I had no answers and often felt envious of others' faith and what looked like mysteriously rich spiritual lives, but I was blessed with an orientation toward meaning-making. By writing poetry, essays, or journaling, I could take in the world around me and explore my inner landscape.

By the end of high school, and thanks to an excellent social science teacher, I knew I was in love with the study of religion—it made me come alive in ways that I had never experienced before. I wandered through bookstores, searching for the next text to read, awash with an uncanny sense of possibility. What was out there, and what would it unlock for me? It was intoxicating, that search for meaning. All those years, my friends gushed about books they loved, but I never fully understood it, that indomitable drive of the voracious reader. But deep in the religion stacks, I learned it in my bones; that sense of wonder and hunger guided me.

I went to college to study religion, and I was formed in a comparative religion department, where I resided in places of intersection. Four religion majors were in my graduating class, two of whom remain my close friends. We adored our professors. They challenged us to think differently, as is their job, but they also took care of us—they accompanied us. They taught me about community and what it means to be seen. While I drew from my Catholic upbringing, that high saturation of ritual, and the fathomless religious imagination, I learned over time that I felt most comfortable in the space between traditions, learning from those different from me. Studying the Yoga Sutras, Zhuangzi, and the Tanakh allowed me to place my family's tradition in conversation with something larger—the human experience, something beyond—and unknowable. I was drawn to the scholarship of the Silk Road, the great meeting place of religion, culture, and commerce. I marveled at how the symbols and images shifted as different voices told Jesus stories from their respective contexts. Years later, I would think back on this time and the malleability of Jesus when diving into the many titles of Mary. Cross-culturally, she can change shape and color to speak personally and authentically to those in her care. Like her son, she is not bound to a single cultural story or a single expression of religiosity. Instead, she is agile—the embodiment of that in-between place. And if that is where the Theotokos (the God-bearer) resides, then that is where God resides, too.

In my fifteen plus years as a higher education chaplain, I have served in a multifaith context where nearly every religious and philosophical offering is open to the community—bringing with it ongoing opportunities for deeper religious literacy and relationship building. This dynamic is one of the many things that makes university life so exhilarating and why I have stayed. Members of our community—including students, faculty, and staff—can explore their traditions and those of others, learn from peers, and get comfortable with being uncomfortable. Like most of their classmates, Catholic students often come to campus with minimal experience in interfaith work. This deficit is understandable. Parishes do not always get a chance to experiment with grassroots interfaith engagement. More often than not, it is a capacity issue. Staff are spread thin and have many pastoral needs to address. In my ministry and activism, I have found that interfaith work is often not seen as a spiritual priority in Catholic settings. Over and over, however, I hear from Catholic students that one of the most meaningful aspects of their time on campus is being part of a diverse religious landscape. Even if they are only tangentially connected to our interfaith work, they are part of a community with an interfaith ethic. This means the values that permeate the chaplaincy are grounded in generous listening, genuine curiosity, and holy envy. Students consistently reflect on how important it is to them that the Catholic community is part of something larger. This larger belonging is a new experience for these young Catholics. And it is transformative.

JULIE'S STORY

A few years ago, our Interfaith Student Council hosted an open mic night. Several Catholic student leaders attended, but when I saw Julie's reflection in the window, walking up the steps of the Interfaith Center, I was surprised and delighted. I had not expected to see her. She wasn't one of our frequent flyers in the interfaith community. Julie was a quiet, highly driven pre-vet student from a relatively homogeneous Catholic community in the United States. She was a committed member of our leadership team, but this was her first interfaith event. She joined me and another student in the second row, and the three of us sat shoulder to shoulder that evening. I knew the other student had prepared to tell a story about his time studying abroad in Italy, but I was shocked when Julie, a self-identified introvert, got up and walked to the microphone. She stood against the backlit wall in her green zip-up hoodie, with her long strawberry hair framing her face. She told us about her deep connection to Saint Francis and how the birds on campus give her pause, connecting her to her faith and her calling. There was the owl that lived by the chapel, the hawk that circled the green, and the cardinals fluttering from branch to branch. Then she set the scene: She worked as a veterinary technician at a practice close to her home. One day, a family she knew came in with their elderly labrador retriever. This dog had been a miracle. Two years before, he had surprised everyone by making a remarkable recovery from illness, but it was clear that he was now at the end of his life. Julie put us in the exam room with her—the dog resting his head in the owner's lap, her gentle pets stroking his coat. Julie was there to be a guiding presence during a humane euthanasia procedure. That was her job. When the veterinarian went out to retrieve the medication, the client turned to Julie.

"This must be so hard for you," the woman said.

Julie was confused. "Hard for me? This must be so hard for you."

"I have been preparing for this," the woman explained, "but you must do this all the time." Then she said it again: "This must be so hard for you."

INTRODUCTION

This woman's expression of care and concern deeply moved Julie. As she addressed us that night at the Interfaith Center, tears welling in her eyes, she pondered, "How can someone be going through something so difficult and then take the time to see it all from another's perspective? Being attentive to *their* pain and *their* grief? And holding it all with such care?"

Julie's questions hung in the air that night. Where does empathy come from, and how might we work to increase empathy in our broken world? How are we called as Catholics to genuinely try to understand the reality of another human being? And have we adequately acknowledged, celebrated, or savored the miraculous nature of connection?

I was in awe of Julie. Her story was a blessing. She had welcomed us into her world—the sustaining beauty of her relationship with creatures and this gritty and profound experience at the threshold of life and death. She allowed us to share in that sense of wonder. When I checked in with her later that week, I asked if she had prepared that story beforehand. It was so well done. The framing, pacing, structure, and depth made it a first-class story that could have easily won a story slam in Boston!

"No," she laughed. "It was just a Holy Spirit moment. Hearing everyone else speak so openly about their lives and cultures was inspiring. It felt like a safe place to try something new."

Reflecting on that night and the sense of wonder in her voice, I am reminded of Rabbi Abraham Joshua Heschel's concept of Radical Amazement. Heschel was a Polish-born twentieth-century American rabbi famous for his contributions to the civil rights movement, his friendship with Rev. Dr. Martin Luther King Jr., and his prolific writings on philosophy and theology. I was on fire when I first encountered his books and was introduced to Radical Amazement. It captured a way of living and being in the world fully oriented toward God's creation and the marvel of existence. In this well-loved quotation, we hear the clarity, urgency, and presence at the heart of Radical Amazement: "Our goal should be to live life in Radical Amazement. . . . Get up in the morning and look at the world in a way that takes nothing for granted. Everything is phenomenal; everything is incredible; never treat life casually. To be spiritual is to be amazed." There are so many threads of Radical Amazement within Julie's story. For one, she began her share that night by revealing her orientation toward wonder, reflecting upon her unique connection to Saint Francis. She saw God wherever she walked, awake to the holy in her midst and receptive to the "Holy Spirit moment," which took courage and trust. The whole night was something of a conversion experience. She decided to turn toward community, attend something new, and share her life, wisdom, and questions—she saw them as worthy of being spoken aloud and inhabiting that sacred space.

When I reflect on the greater circumstances that created that evening—the student leaders who imagined the open mic, the promotion efforts, the thoughtfulness of the hosts to "warm up" the space with dim lighting and chairs in a semicircle—the Radical Amazement continues. So much care went into creating the conditions for that gathering. All that hard work resulted in the space serving as a crucible for connection and meaning-making. Six years later, as she rapidly approaches her graduation from veterinary school, Julie still thinks about that night. And honestly, I do too. I am called to unpack the layers of God's grace revealed in these rich encounters. I am called to lift up the way that other religious/philosophical traditions have enriched my spiritual life. And I am called to celebrate the transformative nature of friendships across traditions.

This book is full of stories like Julie's. I have received permission to share these stories. I have changed names and identifying details to honor privacy. I am deeply grateful for the trust these friends, colleagues, alums, and students have placed in me, offering their lives and stories as sites of study. I hope that in telling these stories, I magnify the wisdom within all of us, but especially in lay Catholics like Julie. Clergy and religious leaders certainly have their role in this work, but layfolk are uniquely poised to step into leadership roles and help build something beautiful. Layfolk are already embedded within their communities. They are involved in public libraries, PTAs, athletics, food pantries, local politics, and social justice organizing. They are already working at intersections of their professional, personal, and spiritual lives. I hope this book inspires us all to lead and follow others as we work to increase empathy and nurture friendships across lines of difference.

IT IS NEVER ABOUT PROSELYTIZATION

Before I go any further, let me be clear that interfaith engagement and friendship are not launching pads for proselytization. We are doing this work to build empathy, nurture meaningful connections, and foster deeper ties within our community contexts. There should be no ulterior motive of converting people to Christianity or luring them into the Catholic Church. Historically, Christians and Catholics have used the pretense of friendship or dialogue to do just that. We must face this deeply troubling past and be aware that when we reach out to others, they may experience some trepidation. Religious minorities are particularly deserving of attention, as they have endured tremendous pressure through the ages to conform to Christianity—politically and theologically. In many instances, such individuals and communities have been faced with the ultimate stakes—conversion or death. We cannot ignore this history, but we cannot allow it to keep us from doing this important work. In the poetic words of seasoned interreligious scholar-practitioner Anantanand Rambachan, "Interreligious friendships will not germinate and flourish in soil saturated with mistrust about mutual intentions."[1] As I will explore in chapter 5, Christians in the United States benefit from our position of privilege in the dominant culture. For this reason, we have a unique responsibility to tend justly to the soil—within ourselves, our parishes, and our broader communities. We must grow roots from a place of honesty, integrity, and trust. I believe that in living creative witness to the Gospel, reaching out in a spirit of humility and genuine curiosity to commune with folks from other religious and philosophical traditions (or no tradition), receiving hospitality, and offering our own, we are embracing the spirit of evangelization. We are spreading the good news of Jesus's radical love ethic and embodying the light of salvation.

TERMINOLOGY

There is much debate around terminology in the field of interreligious/interfaith studies, and there is no consensus. Scholars and scholar-practitioners make convincing cases for using *multifaith*, *interfaith*, *interreligious*, or *pan-religious*. The truth remains—language is imperfect, but areas of disagreement help highlight what is important in the conversation. Each of these terms has its strengths and weaknesses. In different sections of the book, I use language germane to the context. For instance, in chapter 2, which explores conciliar and postconciliar Church documents, I employ the term *interreligious* because that is the language used by the Catholic Church. Throughout the book, however, I more commonly use the terms *interfaith* or *multifaith* because it is the language we use at Tufts University, where I work and where the majority of the stories within these chapters take place. The word *faith* does not resonate with everyone, and of course, it can be a barrier. I can make the same argument as regards *interreligious*—not everyone identifies with the term *religious*, and we should always question who gets to decide what is and is not a religion.

Because I am writing to a Catholic audience, I have decided to use the phrase *religious other* to refer to folks from other religious and philosophical traditions. On the one hand, this term makes me bristle. I do not want to 'other' people. On the other hand, *religious other* serves a function and offers clarity for this project. I do not love this phrase, but it is far superior to another option, *non-Christian*, which inherently centers Christianity. Again, there is no perfect language, so part of our charter is to hold that complexity with care and live into the intersections—the work itself.

CHAPTER OUTLINE

Throughout the book, I weave personal and professional stories into threads of tradition and invite readers to experiment with a variety of spiritual practices and provocations. Some of these exercises are designed for the reader's personal spiritual development; others would work well in a small group or communal setting. Please feel free to engage with these practices however you see fit. You may pause while reading to try them on, return to them later, or use them within a small group.

In chapter 1, I celebrate the rich tradition of spiritual friendship within Christianity. I draw from scripture, the monastic tradition, and contemporary spiritual voices. In chapter 2, I explore how Catholic tradition calls us out of ourselves—through trinitarian theology and the conciliar and postconciliar documents devoted to engagement with other religions. Chapter 3 centers the practice of generous and active listening, which is foundational to this work and to building empathy more broadly. Chapter 4 focuses on expanding our sacramental imagination and unlearning internalized clericalism to participate more fully in the life of the Church. Chapter 5 is concerned with the virtues of nuance, humility, and preparation for Christians to be conscientious players in interfaith settings. Rich in story, chapter 6 magnifies the sacramental nature of interfaith friendship, highlighting six essential components to this work: getting comfortable being uncomfortable, expressing hospitality, creating a container, expanding religious literacy, knowing one's limits, and revelatory experiencing.

It is my hope that this book helps start conversations—within you and within your community. It is not a comprehensive study or a how-to manual. It is but a single entry point. I am confident that in prayer and community, you will find your own.

CHAPTER ONE

Friendship in the Tradition

DRINKING FROM THE WELL

It was getting dark on a cold fall afternoon when we walked from the monastery into Harvard Square. Chris and I had met by chance just a few months before, two youth ministers in rural Maine, both needing a break from our wonderful but utterly exhausting student groups. She was about to start divinity school, and I had just graduated the year before. You might not believe this, but from the moment I saw her, I knew she was mine—or at least, my people. She was chatting with an older woman at the church basement turnover shop. They were human islands in a sea of button-downs and the handmade quilts I had been eyeing since we arrived. After spending the past several days with a crew of fifteen high school boys and two older male teachers, she was a welcome sight. Long French braids peeked out under a bandanna, framing her overall-ed shoulders. She had work boots on and a hoody. We caught each other's eyes in a long, curious gaze. I remember a bemused look on her face when she turned around. "You? Here? Why?" she seemed to ask.

When we eventually did verbalize these questions and received one another's responses with delight, our bond took root. Over the past fifteen years, our friendship has deepened and changed shape as our lives and vocations have continued to unfold. We use different words now to refer to ourselves—pastor, wife, chaplain, mother—but the enchantment remains. That day in Harvard Square, it felt like we were floating above the brick cobblestones, carried along by the Holy Spirit. We were in a state of perpetual wonder, Radical Amazement, reveling at the absurdity of it all—a couple of faithful, "reverently irreverent" Irish American church women in their twenties who met by chance hundreds of miles away from their respective homes. God is good. All the time. All the time.

As we approached the rounded corner by JFK Street, Chris took my arm in hers.

"Have you ever heard of *anamcara*?" she whispered into my ear. "Because that's what I think this is."

She was talking about what we had between us, what we were spontaneously creating. I did not know the term, but when she explained it, I knew what she meant—*the soul friend*. Before the day was through, we stopped by the bookstore, and I purchased a used copy of Irish poet John O'Donohue's beloved book, *Anam Cara: A Book of Celtic Wisdom*. Thus began my introduction to thinking critically about the role of friendship in the spiritual life.

Over the past few years, my studies of friendship and sacramentality have continued. As I go deeper, I find myself surprised by a strange tension. Friendship has long been a central theme in Christianity. Early Church fathers like Augustine, Ambrose, and Saint John Chrysostom committed thousands of pages to the topic. New Testament stories revolve around Jesus and his friends—the disciples. The crux of our tradition, the crucifixion and resurrection of Jesus, are set in motion with his ministry, which so threatened the status quo because he was friends with "undesirables"—tax collectors, sinners, the sick, the forgotten. All this richness fills the ether, but friendship remains an underappreciated thread in Christian spiritual life. I do not fully understand this disconnect, but it has drawn me close and captivated my heart and imagination. In this moment of acuity, when the Covid-19 pandemic has revealed loneliness to be the systemic issue that it is—rather than a personal failing—what would it look like for us as church to embrace and celebrate friendship as the sacrament it is truly, as a doorway to the divine? Sure, there are legitimate questions around how to build meaningful connection (I will get to that later), but I feel like we are sitting here, at the edge of a bottomless well, parched, wishing for our thirst to be quenched, hoping for connection in a turbulent and isolating time. All of this suffering while the tools and insights from our vast tradition are well within our reach.

In this chapter, I seek not to paint a thorough study of friendship discourse within Christianity. That would take volumes! Instead, I dip my vessel into the well, joining in the long lineage of spiritual friendship. Drawing from sacred scripture, monastic tradition, and practical theology, I lift just a sample of friendship touchpoints that capture the beauty and wisdom within. I show how friendship has been in the waters all this time. I invite you to join me and dwell in this part of our shared history and culture as Catholics and to mine it for practical wisdom. As in all chapters, I place these elements of tradition in conversation with my own life and my experience as a chaplain. I explore the desert of loneliness, beloveds who sustain me, and beloveds whose untimely deaths I continue to mourn. As Catholics, we are called to be friends—friends of one another, friends of God, and friends of creation.

FRIENDSHIP IN SCRIPTURE

Mary, Martha, Jesus, and Lazarus

When I turn to scripture, I am overwhelmed by the richness of friendship stories—Ruth and Naomi, Jonathan and David. There are countless references to Jesus's friends—the disciples and all of those with whom he shares a meal, often to the shock and chagrin of others. These are gritty stories of relationships. They depict a multiplicity of intimacies and suggest that spiritual life is richer in the presence of a spiritual friend. One example of friendship that I have spent time praying with and meditating on is that between Mary, Martha, Jesus, and Lazarus. This small circle includes sibling relationships between Martha, Mary, and Lazarus and the friendship between them and their teacher/companion Jesus.

From their appearance in both the Gospel of Luke and the Gospel of John, we can infer that these siblings were significant players in the early Jesus movement. Their story in the fourth gospel, the Gospel of John, is often referred to as "the raising of Lazarus." His resurrection plays a vital role in foreshadowing Jesus's own death and resurrection, but if we jump to the raising of Lazarus, we lose the deep context of this hub of relationships—this friendship web. I love this gospel story. It is a reminder that Jesus and his friends were human beings. The vulnerability and honesty expressed by all three active players—Mary, Martha, and Jesus—speaks volumes to the depth of their connection. The passage begins with Lazarus's illness and places him in relationship to his sisters, Mary and Martha, in their home in Bethany. Mary sends a message to Jesus to let him know that "he whom you love is ill" (John 11:3). In true Gospel of John form, Jesus speaks in near riddles, keeping to the dualistic themes of light and darkness, death and life. His disciples are worried about him going back to Bethany. In the previous chapter, we learn that he had just come from there, and the crowds had turned upon him, threatening him with stones before he retreated to his friend John the Baptist at the Jordan River. Nevertheless, Jesus and the disciples return to Bethany to tend to Lazarus. The passage continues:

> When Jesus arrived, he found that Lazarus had already been in the tomb four days. Now Bethany was near Jerusalem, some two miles away, and many of the Jews had come to Martha and Mary to console them about their brother. When Martha heard that Jesus was coming, she went and met him, while Mary stayed at home. Martha said to Jesus, "Lord, if you had been here, my brother would not have died. But even now I know that God will give you whatever you ask of him." Jesus said to her, "Your brother will rise again." Martha said to him, "I know that he will rise again in the resurrection on

the last day." Jesus said to her, "I am the resurrection and the life. Those who believe in me, even though they die, will live, and everyone who lives and believes in me will never die. Do you believe this?" She said to him, "Yes, Lord, I believe that you are the Messiah, the Son of God, the one coming into the world." (John 11:17–27 NRSV)

This first sentence provides us with the necessary information. The funeral customs are being observed, and Lazarus is indeed dead. He is not transitioning, breathing his last breath. He has been in the tomb for four days. We see from the crowds of fellow mourners how beloved this Bethany family is. Their grief is a public event, with members of the community traveling to comfort them in the immediacy of their loss. The image that remains with me from this section of the scripture is Martha going out to meet Jesus. I feel her sense of urgency. When she sees him, we get a peek into their relationship: "Lord, if you had been here, my brother would not have died" (John 11:21). How human and natural these words sound. These are the words of someone who knows and loves Jesus well. These are also the words of someone in the throes of early mourning. In my own experiences of sudden loss, I have asked this same question: *Where were you, O God, when my beloved passed? Why weren't you there to stop this tragedy from unfolding?* Like many bereaved, I have also asked: *What could have gone differently? What if I had answered the phone? What if they didn't have the money to buy the drugs? What if he never went for that walk? What if? What if? What if?*

This exchange reveals an intimacy and deep connectedness between Martha and Jesus. The commentaries remind us that another central thread of this passage is Martha's proclamation that Jesus is the Messiah.[1] Unlike Peter, who does so after the miracle of the loaves and fishes, Martha's faith needs no grand gesture. Sure, she is confused by what Jesus is telling her, but by the end of the passage, we hear clarity and conviction in her voice. She might not be able to imagine her brother returning to life—who could, really—but she knows who Jesus is and is the first to proclaim this truth.

Four chapters later, Jesus takes a moment to offer *his* clarifying statement. It is the Last Supper. Friends are in an upper room on the precipice of a new reality, a new understanding of discipleship. And it is here that Jesus again frames the heart of his teaching:

> As the Father has loved me, so I have loved you; abide in my love. If you keep my commandments, you will abide in my love, just as I have kept my Father's commandments and abide in his love. I have said these things to you so that my joy may be in you, and that your joy may be complete.
>
> This is my commandment, that you love one another as I have loved you. No one has greater love than this, to lay down one's life for one's friends. You are my friends if you do what I command you. I do not call you servants any longer, because the servant does not know what the master is doing; but I have called you friends, because I have made known to you everything that I have heard from my Father. You did not choose me but I chose you. And I appointed you to go and bear fruit, fruit that will last, so that the Father will give you whatever you ask him in my name. I am giving you these commands so that you may love one another. (John 15:9–17 NRSV)

It is radical for teachers and leaders to express this kind of mutuality and humility. There is the joy of connection and the joy that comes with love. We, in the twenty-first century, know what is about to unfold. This is no sentimental story. It is gritty and real, and sacrifice is embedded within it. Jesus desires humanity to be near him. This desire evokes the giddiness and delight of meeting someone we instantly connect with—like me and Chris. Likewise, it speaks to the wonder that comes when our hearts turn tender for someone who initially pushed our buttons—I'm thinking of my friend Andy, who I met in college. He knows exactly what I'm talking about! It is all good. It is all holy. These seeds of connection, the fruit we bear daily, are part of our call as the baptized. As we begin our reflection on how these stories speak to our own lives, I ask: What fruit are you offering in this world?

Spiritual Provocation

Let us pause and spend time with the second paragraph of this passage. Take a few deep breaths. Feel where your body meets the chair and where your feet meet the earth. When you are settled and have asked God to open your heart to hear the holy word, read and reread these two short sentences: "You did not choose me but I chose you. And I appointed you to go and bear fruit, fruit that will last" (John 15:16). Give yourself five to ten minutes with these words. You may find it helpful to journal, go for a walk, or just sit in silence. If you discover your mind wandering a bit, do not get discouraged. Simply congratulate yourself for noticing and return to these verses.

Remember, Jesus is speaking to the disciples and speaking to you too. Inhabit that space, feel the warmth of these verses wash over you—the way you have been chosen and loved upon—and the challenge of putting that love into action. Feel that sense of call, affirming your fruit-bearing nature and the way your unique gifts have equipped you to contribute to the things that last. May these words of Jesus carry you through this meditation on friendship. May they be our compass in the ongoing work of theological reflection and meaning-making.

The Seventy-Two

In 2019, I piloted a spiritual friendship program for Catholic students at Tufts University. This project grew out of my doctoral research on loneliness in higher education. Over the years, I noticed that some of the isolation students were experiencing on campus was due to a vulnerability problem. They would share things with me that they were too bashful to share with their friends—receiving good news about a fellowship or sad news from family back home. I couldn't quite wrap my head around it. It came from a place of genuine concern—concern around being a burden in one way or another—but it kept them from being authentic with their closest connections. Over dinner one evening, a few student leaders asked me what I was working on in graduate school. When I told them, their ears perked up. Part of my culminating work was creating a practical application for my ministry context. As I mapped out my vision for the friendship program, they eagerly asked if they could participate. I knew then that I was onto something.

I was dreaming of a shared spiritual practice model where participants would commit to spending an hour together each week and a half hour reflecting in a journal. I would send them different prompts and spiritual provocations to explore together during their shared time, and independently, they would reflect on that hour later in the week. How was God speaking to them? What surprised them? What was challenging? The point was for students to get beneath the surface and to talk about the things that matter. Was it a loneliness antidote? Of course not. But it provided an entry point into friendship and an opportunity to build the muscles for meaningful connection. I would later come to think of the content as a scaffolding supporting a kind of reorientation—what would it be like to prioritize relationships and not just tasks, to-do lists, and syllabi? That week, I pulled together a vision, and by the following Sunday, I invited the community to participate in this soft launch of *The 72*. To my great surprise, fourteen students participated that first semester!

I hoped that students might be on a spiritual journey together, learning side by side and trying on different kinds of prayer and reflection. A parallel goal was for them to leave the program with solid active listening skills. I was confident that the Holy Spirit would be there with them in those moments together—and, of course, the bird showed up. During that semester, participants spent their time together on weekly reflective walks (a twist on the Ignatian Examen), sharing meals, contemplating autumnal leaves, and their favorite music. Creating the content in real time was a strange gift.

Each Monday, I would send a spiritual practice to the dyads. In the frenzy of the semester, however, there were weeks when students would reach out to say they couldn't find the practice in their email inbox. Not only had I not sent it, but I had not even written it yet! I would immediately go for a walk and sit down at the computer, drawing inspiration from what was right in front of me—a morning tea ritual, the thresholds on the sidewalk, a poem a friend had sent me the night before. In those moments, I was reminded that we were creating something together, practicing what I preached—finding God in all things. While they were mildly stress-inducing, I secretly loved those emails. The students were really doing these practices! In fact, they seemed hungry for them.

This program has since evolved into an interfaith friendship program, which we now offer to students, faculty, and staff, but the image of the seventy-two has remained with me. I had come up with the name relatively quickly during that mad dash week of planning, but when I prayed with the image more intentionally, I was flush with the Spirit. The story of the seventy-two comes from chapter 10 of the Gospel of Luke. The preceding chapter is chock-full of iconic scenes—the sending forth of the disciples to preach and cure, the loaves and fishes, the Transfiguration, and Jesus teaching his friends the cost of true discipleship. In this context, we encounter the opening story of chapter 10: Jesus sending forth the seventy-two, two by two. Here's how the passage begins:

> After this, the Lord appointed seventy-two others and sent them two by two ahead of him to every town and place where he was about to go. He told them, "The harvest is plentiful, but the workers are few. Ask the Lord of the harvest, therefore, to send out workers into his harvest field. Go! I am sending you out like lambs among wolves. Do not take a purse or bag or sandals; and do not greet anyone on the road.
>
> "When you enter a house, first say, 'Peace to this house.' If someone who promotes peace is there, your peace will rest

on them; if not, it will return to you. Stay there, eating and drinking whatever they give you, for the worker deserves his wages." (Luke 10:1–7 NRSV)

The commentaries tell us that earlier manuscript versions employ the number seventy rather than seventy-two. The thinking is that both numbers symbolically suggest the most comprehensive or all-encompassing reach and may have even been considered interchangeable.[2] In Genesis 10, the Table of Nations lists seventy-two. In the book of Numbers, when Moses is speaking with Elded and Medad at the camp in the wilderness, the Spirit comes "upon the seventy elders. And when the Spirit rested upon them, they prophesized" (Numbers 11:16). These significant numbers, seventy and seventy-two, would have shaken awake early readers and listeners of the story. Their ears would have perked up with the resonance of these symbolically rich numbers—"watch out, something important is about to happen." And so, with the seventy-two (or the seventy), this passage communicates that these pairs are heading into the wilderness, serving the masses—all the nations and all the people.

Jesus entrusts the seventy-two with one another, acknowledging that his charge is no small thing. They are *not* the disciples, Jesus's closest friends who he has been preparing. They are regular human beings like you and me. In today's language, we might say they are layfolk sent forth into the community. The work is hard, and the journey is rugged, but in communion, they are made stronger in will and faith. Bring nothing but trust in one another and confidence in God. He affirms that together on the road, they have companionship, accountability, and the safety of traveling with one another. If you have ever driven cross-country or gone for a long hike, then you know the meandering conversations that unfold on a journey are unlike anything else. Our sense of time shifts, and the hours stretch into one another. Long periods of silence cease to be awkward. In those moments, when we are simply in one another's presence, we live into the great paradoxical truth that, in motion, we are able to cultivate an inner stillness.

When Jesus commissions the seventy-two, he commissions each of us to be in relationship with one another. A friend is a fellow sojourner—a comrade on the spiritual journey, a coconspirator in the vineyard, a partner in the hard work of following Jesus. Friends become our witnesses to life, those whose presence and feedback bring both challenge and comfort. This relationship requires us to slow down, listen deeply, and hold one another accountable. It is about prioritizing relationality, growth, and patience, not perfection. It is about embracing the most distinctive aspect of Christianity—the profoundly interdependent nature of the Holy Trinity. When I think of the seventy-two on the road in pairs, I am reminded of the walk to Emmaus.[3] Of course, the disciples are crushed at that point of the story. They have just lived through the whirlwind drama of Holy Week—Jesus's triumphant return to Jerusalem, his cryptic talk of death, his violent end on a cross, and the empty tomb. Crowds, terror, and heartbreak. As these two distraught friends walk the seven miles between Jerusalem and Emmaus, a stranger joins them. In their grief and humanness, they do not recognize that it is Jesus. It takes his breaking the bread once they arrive to open their eyes and hearts. Like these disciples on the road to Emmaus, the seventy-two are *not* alone. They are accompanied by the Spirit, Jesus himself, Emmanuel—God who is always with us. By extension, we may think of those relationships in our lives as sites of accompaniment. It is never just the two of us. The Holy Spirit resides in the in-between, shaping our connection and guiding us on our shared path.

Soul Friend

The concept of the soul friend has long been at the heart of Christian religious and spiritual life. In the early centuries of the Common Era, the Desert Mothers and Fathers modeled the way of the soul friend. The desire for spiritual companionship brought many Jesus followers to the desert. They longed to be free from obstacles and attachments. They longed for a connection to God and a teacher to show them the way. These desert stories eventually inspired the Celtic Christian religious imagination, which was already steeped in mystery, connectedness, and accompaniment.[4] It is from this tradition that we get the language my friend Chris used that day in Harvard Square—*anamcara*, or soul friend. Theologians, religious professionals, and mystics have gone deep on these topics. Many of their writings have inspired my own spiritual life in profound ways. I do not attempt to recreate those works but lift up some of the powerful threads of this history and spirituality that have shaped how I think of the soul friend and the sacrament of friendship.

I was introduced to the Desert Mothers and Fathers as a first-year college student. These early Christian monastics were called to lives of extreme asceticism, living in caves and cells in the deserts of Egypt and Palestine. They sought to emulate John the Baptist and Jesus on their journeys through the wilderness. For the faithful in the desert, solitude was the key to an authentic connection to God. The Abbas and the Ammas (Fathers and Mothers) modeled this value and guided their followers (Seekers) on their paths, providing words of challenge and encouragement. Several sources from antiquity help us understand this tradition. There are the firsthand accounts of the sayings of the Desert Mothers and Fathers—pithy but rich provocations they offered to their followers—and the synthesized histories like that written (in Latin rather than Greek) by John Cassian in the fifth century.[5] Cassian's writing highlights how much friendship defined the lives of the desert Christians. These compelling stories of the desert elders shaped the religious imaginations of many aspiring Jesus followers. For Cassian, this tradition was rooted in the earliest chapters of the Acts of the Apostles—drawing a straight line between the "pure" mission-driven ministry of those nascent expressions of church and the monasticism that would take shape in the centuries to follow.[6] This connection was essential for Cassian, as it served as a kind of authentication—Cassian equated older with better and truer.[7]

Our Christian tradition is rife with paradoxical truths. God is three, and God is one. Jesus is human, and Jesus is divine. The kingdom of God is yet to come, and the kingdom of God is here and now.

Within the Desert Mothers and Fathers context, we find some of my other favorite ironies—through walking, we cultivate inner stillness, and solitude is the doorway to connection. The desert Christians deeply valued solitude *and* friendship. Perhaps those long stretches of solitude made friendships all the sweeter and more meaningful, or they were seen as two sides of the same coin.[8] After all, they were following in the footsteps of Jesus—someone whose life was defined by both his friends and the times he stepped away to be alone in the wilderness, away from the crowd.

The desert elders served as spiritual mentors or soul friends to the Seekers. They knew from their own experience that human beings can struggle to bring that critical perspective to themselves. We cannot see the things that are most in our way, and often, we are the obstacle itself! However, with the help of an Amma or Abba, a Seeker might gain clarity or insight, allowing them to be more honest with themselves and God. The elders were known to share their own stories in order to normalize the struggle. "Self-disclosure" was a great strength of these relationships as it modeled vulnerability and ongoing learning and formation.[9] In many ways, these relationships foreshadow the model of spiritual direction that we know today. However, as we shall see, there is also a compelling malleability within this system—the teacher/student dyad, the peer-to-peer dyad. While they may take on a different system of power dynamics, the common thread within the soul friend tradition remains a deep reverence for humility and surrender.

In college, my professor invited us to think about the discernment process of the Seekers, especially women who chose to head out into the desert. We know that many Ammas were widows who changed course in their lives—they faced outward to serve others and inward to cultivate a deeper connection with God.[10] Wandering women ascetics were known to shave their heads, dressing as men to protect themselves on the road.[11] This path afforded women a certain autonomy that was impossible in the city and regular Roman society. Countless stories chart the paths of wealthy women who left behind arranged marriages, using their resources to provide for other Seekers and those in need.

I was drawn to this imaginative classroom exercise and jumped to dream of what that kind of discernment process might have sounded like and looked like in antiquity. Of course, my twentieth-century student existence was a barrier to fully comprehending their context, but I, too, was taken by the deep desire to strip away those things that were obstacles in my life. This time was a period when I was on fire for religious experience. I was supple, eager, and hungry for transformation. Through meditation, contemplative practice, writing, running, fasting, and making art with friends, I knew in my bones that I was a theist—that is, I believed in God. I had directly experienced the holy. I could not get into the weeds with any other details, but that much I knew was true. Those moments of deep connection—in solitude and community—changed my religious imagination and life trajectory forever. They helped me to trust in the Spirit and to trust in myself. I was uninterested in answers or naming or claiming a particular destination or goal. It was enough to be on the journey, nourished with small sips of sustenance and guidance every step along the way. I recognized myself in the desert wanderers. While their mentors were far more demanding than my own, and I would never claim to have a fraction of their drive, faithfulness, or discipline, I knew that haunting thirst—for authenticity, proximity to God, clarity of mind, and purity of heart. Honoring their power and relevance to my life felt like an act of reverence. They were not unrelatable spiritual superheroes but human beings. In this practice, I learned that when we place exemplars like the saints or the desert Christians on a pedestal, we strip them of their power and their capacity to shape us and our spiritual lives. After all, how can they inspire us in faith if their stories and practical wisdom are so far out of reach?

Benedictine Oblate Christine Valters Painter has been deeply influenced by the Celtic Church tradition and contemplative practice. She reflects on the connection between Buddhism and the spiritual values of the desert wanderers. She writes,

> The desert monks tried to practice what Buddhists call "beginner's mind." In his Rule, St. Benedict counsels us always to

remember that we are only beginners on the spiritual path. The moment we think we have it all figured out, the further we are from the spiritual path. Conversely, while we may think we have fallen away too far to return, we are also doomed if we never try at all. No matter how far we feel we have strayed from our practice, we are always invited to begin again. Not just each day, but each moment offers us the chance to lay a new foundation.[12]

So much of early monastic spirituality grew out of this kind of rigorous self-examination. Their extreme asceticism and renunciation meant living without the comforts (and distractions) of the city, but this value of stripping away included stripping away things like pretension. While we will dive deeper into beginner's mind in chapter 3, I welcome any opportunity to recalibrate and embrace humility and the value of lifelong learning. As a college student, learning about beginner's mind was so liberating. Like my peers, I spent much time and energy proving my worthiness—through grades, leadership, community service, and athletics. This teaching, however, stressed that the beginner's spirit and perspective illuminate the way. I learned that it is better to embrace oneself as a newbie than to feign or perform expertise.

In her book *The Age of the Saints in Early Celtic Church*, Nora Chadwick explores the connection between the Abba/Amma/Seeker relationships and the tradition of the anamcara. She writes, "In the Celtic Church, as a part of this system of private penance, a monk living in an eremitical life had as a companion, sharing his cell his *anamcara*, or 'soul friend' (Welsh *periglour*) whom he made his confession and who prescribed his penance. The system, which does not appear in the Roman Church of the period, would seem to be a natural development among the desert solitaries of the East."[13] The cellmate was one with whom one could share the burdens on one's heart. The Spirit resided between these two human beings, creating a space for deep reflective practice.

As the Roman Empire conquered Europe, Christianity spread across the continent. However, when it reached the Celts, the rich meeting of these two traditions created a unique expression of Christian spirituality. Saint Brigid exemplifies this hybridity. It is truly remarkable how this single figure embodies multitudes, with overlapping storylines and numerous entry points. Brigid of Kildare was an esteemed abbess and spiritual guide. She founded several monasteries and was known for her hospitality, kindness, and generosity. Her official feast day is February 1. This is the same date for the Celtic festival of Imbolc, the feast for the Celtic goddess Brighid. Imbolc celebrates the transition from winter to spring, symbolized by new life. The word *imbolc* comes from Old Irish, meaning *in the belly*, a reference to lambing and the milk to come. This imagery follows the Saint Brigid narrative. As the story goes, Brigid's mother gave birth on the threshold of a doorway on her way to milk the animals. It was neither winter nor spring, neither day nor night, neither inside nor outside. The story wants us to sit with and in the in-between—and to find value and meaning there. Where does the boundary serve us? Where does it limit us?

In the words of Celtic spirituality scholar Edward Sellner, "Saint Brigit's life stands on the boundary between pagan mythology and Christian spirituality."[14] She lived in the fifth century CE. Because of her connection to birth, however, some stories even have her present at Christ's nativity, serving as midwife to Mary! These narratives are not concerned with linear time. They are concerned with lifting up the gifts that distinguished her ministry—hospitality, compassion, generosity. Within the context of this oral tradition, we see the malleability of culture and story. There is no single source in writing, static in text. Instead, these living, breathing stories were kept alive in and between human beings, shifting and adapting with each retelling.

Anamcara

The gift of the soul friend is the gift of belonging to one another and to creation. They are people with whom we can be honest and walk alongside on this journey—withholding judgment but challenging us to grow in honesty and humility. While the soul friend of the Desert

Christians resembled more of a spiritual direction model (mentor/mentee), the anamcara affords more flexibility, often taking on a dynamic more akin to mutuality. Considering how we are called to surrender to our friends, however, placing ourselves in their hands as heart-bearing monks in the cell, one could argue that we are mentors/mentees to one another—deepening our learning and being together. As I have come to know anamcara in life and study, I am taken by how countercultural this practice can feel in today's frenetic society. The soul friend is not concerned with transactional living or indulging in time scarcity. Instead, the soul friend affords their beloveds spaciousness—uninterested in any end product but deeply invested in the questions on the heart in the present moment and the journey at hand. The soul friend does not expect us to be refined or presentable. They desire us as we are, life on life's terms—#NoFilter.

A famous statement attributed to Saint Brigid often comes up in conversations about anamcara: "A person without a soul friend is like a body without a head." This image conjures an aimless being, devoid of self-reflection and consciousness, unable to connect the senses with the body and the imagination. In my own experience, the soul friend has been vital to helping me see my weaknesses and dream of another story—a healthier, more holistic, more honest way of being. In his practical and poetic book *Soul Friendship in the Celtic Tradition: Ancient Insights for Today*, Anglican priest Ray Simpson writes, "A good soul friend will encourage the Seeker to explore the 'wild places' of her life. God can be encountered in deeper ways, and new wisdom and insight can be gained in these unexplored, challenging areas."[15] I love this passage. The vivid imagery invites me into a place of deep reflection. What are the wild places of your life? What would it feel like to share that with someone else and to see where this untamed landscape might take you?

A Friendship Blessing by John O'Donohue

May you be blessed with good friends.
May you learn to be a good friend to yourself

> May you be able to journey to that place in your soul where there is great love, warmth, feelings, and forgiveness.
> May this change you.
> May it transfigure that which is negative, distant, or cold in you.
> May you be brought in to the real passion, kindship, and affinity of belonging.
> May you treasure your friends.
> May you to be good to them and may you be there for them; may they bring you all the blessings, challenges, truth, and light that you need for your journey.
> May you never be isolated.
> May you always be in the gentle nest of belonging with your anam cara.[16]

Desert of Loneliness

Any practical conversation of anamcara must address the challenges of our present moment. We are living in an age of loneliness. Even with the pandemic helping to normalize this conversation and reveal the systemic dimensions of loneliness, we have so much work to do. It can be enchanting to dream of a soul friend or dive into this mystical tradition's vast landscape, but what if we do not have someone like that in our lives? Would that not make us feel doubly lonely, doubly isolated? I began the chapter with the story of Chris and me, but friendships do not always come through magical meetings. Moreover, holding onto the narrative of a "meet-cute" can sometimes hold us back from reaching out, taking initiative, or appreciating what is already here.

About thirteen years ago, my life was upended by profound loss. Several dear friends succumbed to addiction, and I was able, by the grace of God and family, to extract myself from a dangerous relationship. At that moment, I seriously considered moving to a new city. I felt like I needed to start over and make new connections and new friends. In recovery circles, this is called a "geographic" and is universally frowned upon as an answer. Changing where we live does not erase our issues or dysfunctions; it simply sets a different stage for those patterns to continue. A year later, when I finally settled in my new apartment, I made a concerted effort to build new relationships. I would tell people, "Don't mind me; I'm just out here aggressively befriending." Naming it seemed to lessen the awkwardness! I began volunteering for organizations I had long admired and slowly became a regular in these spaces. I frequented the women-owned bike shop down the street and attended their Friday afternoon hangout sessions. Those gatherings became touch points in my otherwise lonely weeks. Did I leave the bike shop with a whole new family of friends? No. But I did work out some atrophied muscles. Having my life spin out of control had done a number on my spirits and sense of self. Over time, however, I grew in confidence and was less self-conscious. I felt part of my new neighborhood and found great joy in rediscovering this city where I had lived for fifteen years.

I tell this story because we all need reminders that relationships and friendships take work and patience. During different seasons of our lives, it may become easier or more complex, given our contexts. It often requires putting ourselves out there, trying new things, and starting small. When I speak with college students struggling to create community or make friends, I often ask them: *What are you doing to help facilitate connection? Are you inviting folks out to coffee or a walk?* They are not always excited by this provocation. Like all of us, they are afraid of rejection, but the challenge feels more manageable when we map it out in specific steps. These conversations also help disrupt the narrative that if a friendship is to have any future, it must just effortlessly unfold. Sometimes, we need a loving nudge to pay attention to the small moments of connection already in our lives. Not everyone will be our new bestie, but a spirit of intentionality will plant the seeds for greater receptivity. Taking on that posture, we are more generous and openhearted—with ourselves and others—making connections far likelier.

Aelred of Rievaulx's Spiritual Friendship

While the tradition of spiritual accompaniment was rich within the early Desert Mothers and Fathers, Saint Ambrose was one of the first to reflect upon this relationship and deem it virtuous explicitly. This fourth-century Bishop of Milan and Doctor of the Church wrote the earliest text on Christian friendship. He mused,

> What is a friend, in fact, but a partner in love? You unite your inner-most being to his, you join your spirit to his, you blend so thoroughly with him that your aim is to be no longer two but one. You entrust yourself to him as to another self; you fear nothing from him; and you do not ask anything dishonourable from him for your own ends.[17]

Ambrose engaged with the nuances that distinguish friendship—free-willed and steeped in kindness—and saw it as a means to illuminate questions of faith and our connection to the divine. Building upon this tradition, Aelred of Rievaulx, a twelfth-century English Cistercian monk, went even deeper.

Aelred of Rievaulx was a prolific writer, and he concluded his corpus at the end of his life with a dialogical exploration called *Spiritual Friendship*. He drew upon his experience as an abbot for two decades, considering the practical questions that defined his time living in community. For Aelred, spiritual friendship was not just a central element of Christian life but a necessity, the bedrock for spiritual awareness. He wrote from the context of his ministry as a spiritual leader and as someone who knew that unhealthy relationships come at severe costs. Aelred was most concerned with honoring the spiritual richness of healthy friendships. He wanted to lift them up and celebrate their profundity, offering a nuanced approach rather than discouraging intimacy altogether.

Within monastic communities, there had always been suspicion around friendship. Superiors worried that "emotional entanglements" with other members of the community or with folks outside the community could threaten the monk's or nun's spiritual consciousness or devotion.[18] On another level, there were concerns that such a relationship could compromise the greater community. Because monastic spirituality was placed upon a pedestal for laypeople, this message bled out into the world, discouraging the laity from cultivating deep intimacies and vulnerabilities with others.

Within this context we see just how profound Aelred's contributions were to this discourse. He frames three kinds of friendships—carnal, worldly, and spiritual. The first is associated with vice or lustful impulse. It is devoid of thoughtfulness and judgment. The second, worldly, has to do with greed and the desire to gain. It is not trustworthy in spirit as it depends upon iniquity and potential exploitation. By contrast, spiritual friendship is an expression of mutuality. It is the response to Jesus's call in the Gospel of John "to go and bear fruit, fruit that will last. . . . I am giving you these commands so that you may love one another." (John 15:16–17, NRSV) Aelred doubles down on this passage, teaching us that being friends with one another is being friends with Jesus.

In the second book of *Spiritual Friendship*, Aelred speaks with Walter, a monk in his community. Walter and his questions function as a way to unpack the conversation and dig into the nitty gritty of relationships. He is a stand-in for the reader. As he explains to his superior, Walter wants to open up but is curious about what he will gain. He wants to know more about the "purposes and rewards" of friendship. Aelred first humbles himself to the sheer magnitude of this challenge and then unpacks friendship's riches. He explains to Walter,

> The wise man says "a friend is medicine for life." What a striking metaphor! No remedy is more powerful, effective, and distinctive in everything that fills this life than to have someone to share your every loss with compassion and your ever gain with congratulation. Hence, shoulder to shoulder, according to Paul, friends carry each other's burdens, though they each bear their own bruises more lightheartedly than their friend's.

> Thus friendship *by dividing and sharing makes prosperity more splendid and adversity more tolerable.*[19]

For Aelred, friendships serve a real function. They offer tangible benefits. They make the light brighter, the gnarly thicket more bearable. A spiritual friend magnifies God's grace. A spiritual friend expresses God's presence on earth, the Holy Spirit in action in and between us. This passage shows Aelred's awareness of and deep appreciation for the critical role of the confidant on life's journey. They are a gift *to and from* God, expanding our capacity for life. Spiritual friendship is a verb, an unfolding of gifts, a beholding of holiness and tenderness. We cannot reach a place of authenticity without embracing vulnerability.

While this above passage offers a systematic framing of the advantages of friendship, Aelred's final words incorporate Christ in a truly moving way. His expression of embodiment and powerful poeticism beckons us to engage with our sacramental imagination. The spiritual friend emboldens our experience of the Eucharist—bringing it out into the world of our relationships, thereby integrating Christ fully into our daily lives. As regards orienting ourselves toward one another, and thus Christ, Aelred writes,

> Sometimes suddenly, imperceptibly, affection melts into affection, and somehow touching the sweetness of Christ nearby, one begins to taste how dear he is and experience how sweet he is. Thus rising from that holy love with which a friend embraces a friend to that with which a friend embraces Christ, one may take the spiritual fruit of friendship fully and joyfully into the mouth, while looking forward to the abundance in the life to come.[20]

Aelred explicitly connects the love of Christ and the love of friends. Not only that, but his evocative language brings us face-to-face with the embodied reality of our existence. It is sensuous. We are sensuous. The call to savor the fruits of friendship on our tongues is a call to open ourselves up to the holy, to the gifts of one another, to be transformed by the sacramental encounter. Our incarnational faith does not always engage the body and our sensuous existence with as much enthusiasm as I hear in Aelred's closing words. Taken in conversation with the body-denying sensibilities of the desert elders and monastic culture more generally, it is all the more prophetic. His enfleshed imagery reminds us to behold God and all of creation and to remain awake to the diversity of ways our bodies afford us experiences of the divine.

Friends of God

I hesitate to make clear distinctions between being friends with human beings and being friends with God because these relationships are deeply intertwined. We see that in Aelred and the Gospel of Matthew, when Jesus explains to the disciples in the Judgment of the Nations, "Truly I tell you, just as you did for the least of these, you did it to me" (Matthew 25:40, NRSV). Caring for others is caring for Christ. Being friends with human beings is being friends with Christ.[21] In his beautiful little book, *A Friendship Like No Other: Experiencing God's Amazing Embrace*, Jesuit priest William A. Barry captures this both/and. He writes, "Just as human friendship entails becoming a friend of my friend's friends and family, so, too, becoming God's friend involves accepting God's other friends, at least in principle. Mind you, God's other friends are potentially all the people on the planet. So my joy, my fulfillment, my salvation consists in opening myself to friendship with God and with every man, woman, and child ever created. At the least, I must be open to conversation with God about having such a large heart."[22] Expanding our imaginations around God's friends requires expanding our hearts. There is no pretension here, no Christocentric self-aggrandizement, but an invitation to take in and celebrate creation holistically. I appreciate how Barry acknowledges the demanding nature of this spiritual posture. Aspiring to live with this orientation to the world is no small thing. Instead of being overwhelmed by the challenge of honoring all people as God's friends, Barry invites us to honor our humanness and limitations by bringing God into the conversation.

One of my favorite times to chat with God is on my commute to campus. I wait until I have been driving for a while in silence and then I begin my prayer, speaking out loud to God in the car as I would with a friend in the front seat. I take a deep breath and get real: "God, I really *want* to be more gracious and big-hearted, but, honestly, it is hard. Sometimes, I feel at capacity, as if I need to protect my time and energy. Other times, I fall into patterns of judgment that I know are less than charitable—but I do it anyway. I don't know why. Maybe it gives me some instant self-satisfaction, or it is just a muscle memory I'm not proud of. Help me be more generous all around—with my time and heart." These conversation sessions with my friend in the car remind me that prayer does not change the outer world. It is not about hoping for miraculous gifts from the sky that will instantly heal our broken but beautiful world. Instead, through prayer, *we* are changed—our internal landscape and our orientation in the world. On my way to the chapel on Sunday afternoons, my well fills up on the drive. I feel unburdened. I am reminded that I never do anything alone. As my friend Heather and I often remind each other, "The bird don't call out sick." Being vulnerable with God in this way allows us to be more honest with ourselves. Only when we are vulnerable with one another and with God can we get to a place of authenticity in our relationships and spiritual life.

For some readers, it might be new territory to think of God as a friend. Perhaps this feels irreverent or lacking the appropriate degree of gravity or deference. You may have been taught to fear God, which would make the friendship model even more alarming. In my conversations with students, this barrier often comes up. The distinction between creator and created is real, and for some, the suggestion of a mutual relation can feel at odds with the tradition of one's childhood. In his book *Friends in Christ: Paths to a New Understanding of Church*, Brother John of Taizé gives voice to this dynamic. He is writing from within the Taizé community, which is an international ecumenical monastic movement in France that has thought deeply about the transformative power of friendship across differences. Brother John offers a way into this middle path. He writes, "Without lowering the Song of God to the status of a 'buddy,' we can through prayer, grow in the conviction of a supporting and loving presence that never abandons us, to which we can constantly entrust our deepest sorrows and joys, and which helps us to find our way through the labyrinth of a world alienated from its deepest roots."[23] I appreciate the care with which Brother John frames this entry point. We can at once understand the richness of God as a friend and operate from a place of appropriate reverence.

Sometimes, we must also address how we perceive ourselves and if that perception is part of our limitations in spiritual life. Some of my students have been taught to think lowly of human beings. Sadly, this has translated to questioning or denying their worthiness. With the growing awareness of the mental health crises in young folks, this kind of theology feels all the more inappropriate and damaging. We have much work to do to support the process of unlearning. Moving toward a life-giving posture is no small thing. And because I could not say it any better than Father Barry, "I urge you to ask God to purge from your heart the vestiges of fear that produce feelings of insignificance and unworthiness. You do God no favor by thinking stingily or meanly about the person who is the apple of God's eye—you."[24]

While there are no doubt pockets of enriching and innovative Catholic religious education in the United States, we have much work to do in ongoing adult spiritual formation. This means we must equip layfolk with a foundation and the opportunities to mature spiritually as they move through adulthood. Without this scaffolding, it is easy to get stuck in childish notions of God—a superhero, or Santa Claus, who grants wishes. Part of my role as a chaplain is to invite students to stretch their spiritual imaginations and to grow into a mature spirituality that pushes back on these two-dimensional ideas. Our ministry invites them into new ways of thinking and being. This work is hard. The familiar, in all its limitations, can be so comforting. Moreover, a spiritual journey is not like a syllabus. There is no checklist to lull us into a sense of a job well done. Getting comfortable with uncertainty and unknowing takes time and patience. It is helpful to remember, however, that even monastics who devote their lives to God struggle to find their way. Twentieth-century American Trappist monk Thomas Merton captures this beautifully in the prayer that is attributed to him: "My Lord God, I have no idea where I am going. . . . I will not fear, for you are ever with me, and you will never leave me to face my perils alone."[25]

As Merton and Brother John affirm, being friends of God means knowing wholeheartedly that God will never leave us to face our perils alone. We may not have all the answers or even know what our destination might look like—or if there is one—but that spirit of accompaniment is transformative. Our friend is with us, here to call us to account, listen to what is on our hearts, challenge us to grow in new directions, and be open to transformation.

A few years ago, I met regularly with a young woman who was discerning initiation into the Catholic Church. She had been baptized in another branch of Christianity but had found meaningful community and connection in a local parish she had started attending back home. It is rare to hear a young person speak so candidly about their relationship with God. This woman, however, spoke with deep affection and intimacy. At times, I did a double take. Was she speaking of a mentor or spiritual director? In some ways, she was! As we met over coffee and delicious sweet treats at the bakery across the street from my office, I listened in awe—inspired by her clarity and trust. What I heard in those conversations was a deep sense of being held. She was in discernment about which church to join, and that was no light matter, but her connection to God was not up for debate. In all its uncertainty, the journey feels more doable and less daunting when we know we are not alone. As her chaplain, I walked alongside her for those few months, but she was well on her way, nurturing her deep friendship with the holy.

What stood out to me about this woman's spiritual life was her regular connection to prayer. The monastics in my life have taught me a lot about the transformative power of rhythmic living. Having a scaffolding allows one to remain near and in deep awareness of God's omnipresence. This woman was living out this practical wisdom as a first-year college student. As Brother John of Taizé explains, "Friendship is characterized by attentiveness to the other person and in our relationship with God; this is what we call personal prayer.... When prayer becomes part of the warp and woof of existence, it ultimately comes to define who we are. In this respect, a few minutes a day of intimacy with God, regularly maintained, accomplishes more than short-lived bursts of enthusiasm that inevitably become nothing more than good intentions."[26] This faithful showing up, if even for a few minutes a day, steadily adds to a foundational relationship—we might think of it as building rapport with God.

We Are God's Friend Too

One of my favorite Gospel moments is Jesus appearing to the disciples in chapter 21 of the Gospel of John. I often use this passage when introducing groups to Ignatian Contemplation (also known as Imaginative Prayer or Composition of Place). This spiritual practice invites us to sink deeper into the specific context of a Scripture story. We engage our senses in this contemplative exercise, placing ourselves in the scene and calling attention to the embodied experience of the characters—those explicitly mentioned or those whom we read into the text. When we open ourselves up to encountering familiar stories intentionally and imaginatively, the spirit blesses us with fresh perspectives and insight. In this part of the fourth gospel, the disciples are grief-stricken and probably afraid that they have raised the attention of the authorities. Like the disciples walking to Emmaus, there's a shadow of fear that they might be next. Simon Peter turns to his friends and says, "I'm going out to fish" (John 21:3). This simple sentence holds so much. It is as if they do not know what to do with themselves, so they do what they know best. If you have ever experienced profound loss or a time of crisis, perhaps you know what it is like. Sitting together with your fellow bereaved, not knowing what to do. And then, thanks be to God, someone has an idea. Again, how human, how relatable.

The five of them go fishing all night, but they catch nothing. The passage continues:

> Just after daybreak, Jesus stood on the beach; but the disciples did not know that it was Jesus. Jesus said to them, "Children, you have no fish, have you?" They answered him, "No." He said to them, "Cast the net to the right side of the boat, and you will find some." So they cast it, and now they were not able to haul it in because there were so many fish. That disciple whom Jesus loved said to Peter, "It is the Lord!" When Simon Peter heard that it was the Lord, he put on some clothes, for he was naked, and jumped into the sea. But the other disciples came in the boat, dragging the net full of fish, for they were not far from the land, only about a hundred yards off.
>
> When they had gone ashore, they saw a charcoal fire there, with fish on it, and bread. Jesus said to them, "Bring some of the fish that you have just caught." So Simon Peter went aboard and hauled the net ashore, full of large fish, a hundred fifty-three of them; and though there were so many, the net was not torn. Jesus said to them, "Come and have breakfast." (John 21:4–12)

There is so much richness in this passage. In some reflection sessions with students, we have focused on what it is like to toil for so many hours with nothing to show for it. We reflect on the deep trust needed to cast our hopes into the darkness—faith in the unknown fathoms. On other occasions, we have sat with possible emotional responses the disciples might have had to that pesky stranger on the beach insisting they throw their nets over again. For this reflection, however, I will focus on Simon Peter and the moment he "jumped into the sea."

When I read this passage with small groups, someone always points out that it sounds like Simon Peter was fishing naked and chose to put on clothes before swimming in the sea. It is indeed noteworthy! Some read this detail as an expression of his wanting to be appropriately respectful to Jesus. Others find resonance in his shame of betrayal and covering up, like Adam and Eve in the garden of Eden. Like us, Peter still has a lot to learn. But we can learn from his leap. I find the visuals so compelling. Sometimes, I imagine it as the elegant jump of someone who has done this many times. On other days, it reads like a frenzied near-disaster that almost capsizes the boat. Either way, the sense of urgency remains.

Spiritual Provocation

I invite you now to take a moment and dream with me and this passage. Take a few deep breaths to settle the spirit and remind yourself that you are in God's presence. Ask the Holy Spirit to open your imagination and heart. You may close your eyes or soften your gaze, whatever will help you be present and grounded. Enter the scene and see where it takes you. Inhabit one of the players in the scene—a disciple, Jesus, someone in the distance watching the whole peculiar event unfold. What do you hear, smell, taste, touch, and see? Reread the passage (John 21:4–12) and pay close attention to what you observe. When you make it to the end of the passage and smell the breakfast cooking on the beach, please return to this page and continue reading.

(Pause.)

Welcome back. You are smelling the breakfast on the beach, but I invite you to rewind to the moments on the boat. Peer across the surface of the water. Perhaps you see a reflection from the sky or notice ripples in the tide. Now imagine that it is God in the boat, and upon recognizing you on the shore, it is God who erupts with delight and wonder. Behold, the Most Holy is jumping into the water, eagerly swimming to greet you, yearning only to be close to you. Feel the sense of urgency and joy. What is it like feeling so desired, so cherished, so loved? Can you imagine, can you taste, for just a fleeting moment, the depth of God's love for you? This is the love of a friend who is always near, always ready for you to answer the phone, giddy to receive your text, ready for an adventure, or standing with their arms outstretched so you, in your weariness, can rest your head upon their chest. May the truth of God's delight in you bring you abiding comfort and solace.

New ways of imagining and experiencing God can be so refreshing, but of course, we must acknowledge that the fullness of God is beyond our capacity to imagine. Using any image will inevitably fall short of the breadth of God's grace and love. Still, as human beings living with the limitations of language, we look for other ways to communicate and understand the holy. Through fragments like God leaping out of the boat to swim toward us in a hasty greeting, us leaping out of the boat to swim toward God in swift delight, to God being the fire and fish that will nourish us in our time of fellowship, we expand our horizons of understanding the many facets of our sacred wellspring.

The Gift of Being Seen

Throughout the examples of this chapter, a common thread has surfaced: Being genuinely seen is transformative. Jesus sent out the seventy-two, knowing that what they needed already resided within them. Mary truly sees that Jesus is the Messiah. She and her sister Martha's grief is indeed seen by the community that has rallied to support them. The Seekers in the desert stripped away everything to get to the essence of self—placing themselves in the hands of the Ammas and Abbas, whom they trusted. The spiritual friendship of Aelred and the anamcara tradition are rooted in the transformative process of coming to know one another with no pretense or mask.

The gift of being seen has profoundly shaped my understanding of what it means to be part of a community of care.

In October 2008, I lost my dear friend E to an overdose. I was devastated. His passing was a landmark moment in my life, the first death of a peer I knew intimately and, sadly, the first of many in my circle of friends. Because he was neither a family member nor a significant other, the profundity of my grief confused people. There was this underlying assumption that the death of a friend should not affect someone as much as his death was affecting me. At the time, I worked at a high school, and several people encouraged me to "throw myself into my work." While I knew intellectually that this was a coping mechanism many employed in such moments, I found the advice unhelpful and mildly infuriating. E was a creative partner with whom I cooked meals and made art. The hours we spent together often felt enchanted—we rarely had a plan; we just wandered the city sidewalks, taking in the beauty and the grit. Our conversations felt holy and raw. There was a part of me that only surfaced when in his presence—when it was just the two of us. But it wasn't all easy or pretty. Debilitating migraines plagued him, and at times, he was erratic. He was suffering in many ways he did not share with me, but I loved him, and I loved what we created together.

Nine months after E passed, at the start of my summer vacation, I began attending daily Mass at the parish in my neighborhood. The other parishioners were all retired folks who lived across the street and had attended this parish for decades. It was a core group of ten or twelve elders, and I was moved by their connection to one another and their shared connection to the lectionary. Their pastor called them his "Morning Glories" as they began each day together. They lived out the drama of daily scripture passages like a book club exploring a serial novel! After Mass one morning, the Morning Glories headed home, and I stood on the church's steps talking with the pastor. I began to tell him about E. He stood there with me, listening intently as I told stories and reflected on my sadness. When I paused for a moment, he shook his head and said something that changed me: "Life's a bitch sometimes, isn't it?"

I was at once shocked and relieved. I was shocked by his swearing and that a few words could bring such comfort. I felt seen and instantly less alone. I felt understood. It reminded me of divinity school and learning to study and pray with the psalms—that powerful reminder that nothing I am experiencing is new. Human beings have felt this way before, many times over. In his use of the word "sometimes," I heard, "this too shall pass." I took a deep breath, relieved that I wouldn't always feel as I did then.

When I think about the role of friendship in spiritual life, I think about that conversation on the steps of the church. I did not know that priest well, but this interaction set me on a path of healing and recovery. His kindness and empathy communicated God's grace in a moment of suffering. He took the time to listen and affirm my reality, which made all the difference. Shortly after that, this priest put me in touch with his friend, a Sister of Saint Joseph and a spiritual director. She sat with me during those few short summer months, creating a container to explore my grief. Sitting in her office, I felt seen and valued. She validated the double harm I suffered—E's sudden passing and how our culture had rendered my loss essentially invisible. In the years since, I have seen this experience as profoundly revealing—a case study of the lack of reverence and appreciation our culture has for friendship and the lasting impact that friendship can have on the spiritual life.

Spiritual Provocation

Think back to a time when someone's actions or words helped you to feel genuinely seen, heard, or understood. Maybe it was a friend, family member, stranger, or someone you just met. If you need space or time to access those parts of yourself, journal for ten minutes or take a walk—physically or mentally by daydreaming. When you arrive at your memory, place yourself back in the moment. Dwell there for a bit. In the spirit of Saint Ignatius's Composition of Place, engage your senses. What sounds do you hear in the physical context of your memory? What does it taste like, look like, smell like? How did your body respond when you felt seen, heard, and understood? When you are ready, dwell with an excerpt of this psalm.

> O Lord, you have searched me and known me.
>
> You know when I sit down and when I rise up;
>   you discern my thoughts from far away.
> You search out my path and my lying down,
>   and are acquainted with all my ways...
>
> For it was you who formed my inward parts;
>   you knit me together in my mother's womb.
> I praise you, for I am fearfully and wonderfully made.
>   (Psalm 139 1:1–3, 13–14 NRSV)

Knowing what it was like to be understood and known by a human being, can you imagine the magnitude of God's love—how God sees, knows, and understands you? These tastes of wholeness and connection are beautiful and transformative, and they are, of course, just a taste. How might you bring the gift of being seen into your day-to-day life? Are there folks in your community that are invisible? How might God be calling you to be a friend to others?

CHAPTER TWO

Interdependence and Difference

In November 2007, I traveled with a group of Catholic campus ministry colleagues and high school students to Fort Benning, Georgia, to protest the violence perpetrated by graduates of the School of the Americas. Those five days were full of powerful moments and prophetic witness. It was my introduction to the Catholic peace movement. I was heartened and deeply inspired by walking beside countless orders of religious sisters, university students, professors, religious professionals, Catholic Workers, and homegrown peace activists. The energy was palpable and the mood somber, but I felt an invigorating spirit of solidarity in the atmosphere. My dear friend Heather Angell, a fellow campus minister, spent those days continually running into friends, people with whom she had made this pilgrimage just a few years before. One of those folks was a Jesuit priest whom she had come to know well during their time together at university. Before he headed to the front of the procession, with a strong likelihood he would be arrested, he turned to her, bowed his head, and said, "Angell, bless me, won't you?" I watched as my friend took his head in her hands and closed her eyes. As someone always hungry to understand prayer—desperately curious to know what it sounds like and feels like—I wished I could hear her voice. What does it sound like to send forth a beloved in preparation for arrest? What does it sound like for a laywoman to bless a priest?

Opening her eyes, she traced a small cross upon his forehead with her thumb. It was an ordinary moment, yet it changed how I thought about pastoral authority, humility, and the Holy Trinity.

As a Catholic in a multifaith context, the Holy Trinity centers and defines my posture working with and among religious others. I am captivated by this part of our tradition—the Trinity and marking oneself with the sign of the cross—and how it communicates a deep value, tracing it quite literally onto our bodies. I have, at times, felt like a fish swimming in the Trinitarian waters. It has been so much a part of my life and landscape that I have not fully comprehended its beauty and power. However, when I take a step back and contemplate how the Holy Trinity calls me into new spaces and to live a life of intersections and interdependence, I am filled with clarity. This chapter explores this deep connection, placing trinitarian theology in conversation with personal spiritual reflections and multifaith chaplaincy. How are we called to be in relationship across difference? How might the Holy Trinity be our guide in interfaith work? In the second half of the chapter, I turn to conciliar and postconciliar documents that explicitly lift up and celebrate relationships with folks from other religious and philosophical traditions. With these streams of theology and praxis—the Holy Trinity and interreligious dialogue—I celebrate how the Catholic tradition invites us to connect across difference.

THE HOLY TRINITY IN CONTEXT

The Trinity is all about interdependence in difference. It is rooted in the dynamism, movement, and right relation of the fellowship of the three Persons of the divine—God the Father, God the Son, and God the Holy Spirit. I employ the term "Person" in the spirit of Brazilian theologian Leonardo Boff, who defines "Person," or the Greek *hypostasis*, as "that which is distinct in God, the Father, the Son, and the Holy Spirit; the individuality of each Person who simultaneously exists in itself and in eternal communion with the other two."[1] Concurrent distinction and interdependence is vital to appreciating the implications of this teaching for our lives. The triune God is social. The triune God is a community, interdependence itself, and because we are made in God's image, we, too, are social, communal, and interdependent.

For all its centrality, the Trinity is rarely drawn upon and explored in meaningful, creative, or joyful ways. Perhaps it is overwhelming—the paradox and the mystery. Its complexity means that most language used to describe its nature diminishes or limits it in unorthodox ways. The Trinity can also feel elusive, even as it grounds our worship and prayer. As Catholics, we enter sacred spaces, blessing our bodies with the three Persons. Stations of Holy Water wait at the threshold, beckoning us to dip our fingers. We interrupt the water's surface, marking our bodies with the same substance used by countless others to mark theirs. When we make the sign of the cross, we touch our head, chest, and shoulders. It is called "the sign of the cross," but depending on how far down the chest one marks "the Son," it can look more like a triangle than a cross. Early Christians began this practice without speaking aloud the Persons of the Trinity. Over time, however, this practice has evolved and shifted. Crossing oneself transposes the reality and profundity of the three Persons onto our body. It points toward the deep, interdependent relationship between our minds, hearts, bodies, and spirits, marking us with a collective identity spanning centuries. We are connected to those who have come before us and those who live worldwide. We are connected to creation. This interconnection reflects something deeper about the nature of God and what it means to be a human being on this earth.

The doctrine of the Trinity is a subset of the fullness of our understanding of divinity, but the Trinity is also understood through its direct revelation in history. As Leonardo Boff writes, "We must always distinguish between the reality of the Trinity and the Doctrine of the Trinity. . . . The Trinity is not revealed as a doctrine but as a practice: in the deeds and words of Jesus and in the actions of the Holy Spirit in the world and in the people."[2] Catholic theologians and mystics guide this chapter, bringing practice and doctrine into conversation with one another. When we live the truth of the Trinity, it challenges and changes us. Our hearts and imaginations expand when we are actively learning and experiencing our interdependence with all of creation.

HEAD AND SHOULDERS: A THEOPOETIC OF THE HOLY TRINITY

Crossing oneself is a site for theological wisdom and deep reflection. To focus on this embodied expression of trinitarian theology, we are reminded of the earliest Jesus followers, who were experiencing God in and between one another. Their encounters with the holy, as recounted in the Acts of the Apostles, were wondrous, mysterious, and sometimes terrifying. These human beings sought to give words to such experiences and employed symbols to communicate their stories more effectively. Catholic theologian Elizabeth Johnson succinctly expresses this ongoing relationship between human experience and Church teaching. As if to offer a reality check on parts of the tradition that we now somewhat take for granted, Johnson writes, "The point of all these theological constructions is to give voice to fragmentary saving experiences as experiences of God, in the living tradition of the Christian story."[3] Johnson's words remind us that the story is ever unfolding within each of us, in our bodies, in our relationships—our joys and our sufferings. Looking back upon early Christians, we may be surprised to learn that it was not until the Council of Nicaea in the fourth-century that the Trinity was formally written into doctrine, as visioned and grounded by Augustine. Early references to the act of imposing crosses upon one's body teach us that Christians used their bodies to mark the reality of the Holy Trinity. Well before scribes, councils, and heresies solidified a doctrine, the power of beholding and embodying the Trinitarian interdependence took precedence. Writing about this theology is to attempt to pin it down—something that conflicts with the inherent movement and creativity most associated with the Trinity. Language falls short, as it often does, and yet I do my best to reflect on how it looks and feels when we mark our bodies with this foundational and incarnational truth of our tradition.

Crossing oneself is as rich as it is pervasive. As with many aspects of ritual, however, it is easy for this part of religious observance to become rote—something we do because we do it, without much cause for pause. We may cruise through the motions, marking the head, heart, and shoulders without considering what we are really doing. Perhaps we are running late for Mass and eyeing the pews for an empty seat or just so used to the movement that we fail to acknowledge the significance of each stop along the way—the Father, the Son, and the Holy Spirit. Some Catholics think of this act as an intersection point of Jesus's commandments: the vertical motion being the love of God and the horizontal the love of neighbor. These lines mark the meeting of our breastbone, just above our hearts. It is a moment of cruciform intersection—the tolling of a bell that rings within and throughout the body of Christ, making the invisible reality of God's life in us visible.

The slight movement of Heather's thumb transposed this truth upon her friend. This everyday act calls to the more formalized rituals of the Sacraments of Baptism, Confirmation, Holy Orders, and Anointing, wherein a small cross is drawn upon the forehead by the celebrant (and on the hands as well in the Anointing). When it comes to these Sacraments, the celebrant may speak aloud different words, depending on the context and occasion, but the thread is there—there is a deep commitment to tracing the cross and, thus, the Trinity on the body. When we prepare ourselves for the gospel in liturgy, three small crosses come into conversation with one another as we draw them upon our heads, lips, and hearts. In doing so, we pray that God may open our minds to hear the word, our lips to proclaim the word, and our hearts to receive the word. These practices remind us—and our bodies—that the triune God is actively at work, inscribed upon us, holding us, and always in motion in and between us.

Tertullian, a church father of the third century, famously described the integration of the sign of the cross into the daily lives of early Christians. He said, "In all our travels and movements, in all our coming and going out, in putting on our shoes, at the bath, at the table, in lighting our candles, in lying down, in sitting down, whatever employment occupies us, we mark our forehead with the sign of the cross."[4] Tertullian's words offer a glimpse into another time, when the practice was woven into the seemingly mundane thresholds of the day. The cross was drawn upon the body in moments of pause and movement, in caring for one's body, and in exchanging time for money. He was speaking of an orientation toward the Trinity, an orientation toward sacrament within the ordinary and unspectacular moments of the day. These words suggest a fundamental integration of faith into life, reflecting the proverbial seamless garment. The attention to the thresholds is an invitation to stay awake to the border crossings in our lives—literal and metaphorical. The practice of blessing oneself has since shifted from a forehead cross to a head/heart/shoulder movement. Many contemporary American Catholics only cross themselves bookending prayer or when entering a sanctuary. Tertullian describes a theology that was not yet doctrine but a central and defining element of lived religion. This snapshot shows early Christians threading their days with disruptive action. I use the word "disruptive" to convey the genuine rupture of consciousness and the transformation of physical space that goes into drawing a cross upon one's forehead. It takes a continuous sacramental consciousness to engage the rhythms of the day with this kind of intentionality.

The Trinity is, of course, a mystery, but Franciscan friar Richard Rohr offers an exciting point to explore. In his book *The Divine Dance*, Rohr recenters our relationship to mystery. He writes that it is not that we cannot understand the mystery but that we are forever understanding it. As regards the Trinity, he says, "It is something that you can *endlessly understand*! There is no point at which you can say, 'I've got it.' Always and forever the mystery *gets you*!"[5] For

Rohr, the ambiguity, the constant shifting, and ongoing experiences of awe, clarity, and confusion define the Trinity. His gracious, spacious, and joyous reading of our practical relationship to the Trinity grounds and affirms our diverse experiences, creating opportunities for mystery and spiritual journey to inform one another mutually. He invites us to celebrate our growing and changing relationship with doctrine and practice, allowing for complexity and continual rediscovery. This posture enables our lives—our joys, sufferings, and stories—to define and redefine our understanding of the mystery, an acceptance and celebration of its deep-seated relationality. I love how Rohr's work is infused with a spirit of humility. We cannot know it all, and truly, what would be the fun of that? The ongoing, lifelong learning of being in relationship to this two-thousand-year-old tradition means that there is always more to come. Patience, spaciousness, and genuine curiosity can guide us in learning our tradition and learning with and from others about theirs.

Spiritual Provocation: Sites of Meeting

With the Trinity in mind, I invite you to try this mindfulness practice rooted in intersection. You may choose to head out for a walk or traverse a well-known path in your imagination. Begin by centering yourself with a few long, deep breaths. Ask God to open your heart and mind. On your walk, pay special attention to the thresholds—doorways, passing strangers on the sidewalk, street corners, stoplights. Study the architecture of the landscape. Notice how our world is full of sites of meeting. Encounter it with a fresh perspective. What did you observe? Did anything surprise you? Was there a favorite "site of meeting" on your walk? Why were you drawn to it?

Take a few more deep breaths and end with this question: How might you bring these reflections with you the next time you traverse this path or when you are somewhere new?

Close by giving thanks to God.

THE DANCE OF THE TRINITY

Perichoresis is defined as being-in-one-another, "permeation without confusion."[6] The term is thought to have been first used by Gregory of Nazianzus, the fourth-century Archbishop of Constantinople, as a means to capture the dynamism of Jesus as fully human and fully divine. In the years that followed, this term would be employed in Trinitarian theology as regards the three Persons. Theologians have struggled to wrestle this term into a single definition, finding greater comfort and precision in using metaphor to convey its significance. Many have relied upon the image of the divine dance to capture the creative movement and mutuality of the Trinity. Catholic theologian Catherine Mowry LaCugna observes that "choreography suggests the partnership of movement, symmetrical but not redundant, as each dancer expresses and at the same time fulfills him/herself toward the other. In interaction and inter-course, the dancers (and the observers) experience one fluid motion of encircling, encompassing, permeating, enveloping, outstretching. There are neither leaders nor followers in the divine dance, only an eternal movement of reciprocal giving and receiving, giving again and receiving again. . . .The image of the dance forbids us to think of God as solitary."[7]

The single motion suggests timelessness and a seamless primordial creative energy. We must stretch our imaginations in our attempts to behold the divine dance. With no leader or follower, no end, and no beginning, the choreography of the Trinity is antithetical to the nature of our society, our Church. It does not operate within the limitations of our world, and so we are challenged to expand ourselves—opening the contours of our inner landscape to grow in imaginative capacity. LaCugna's imagery plants the seeds for the Catholic religious imagination and reminds us of Jesus's profoundly countercultural message. We should not be surprised that the whole of the three Persons mirrors the spirit of inversion and innovation preached by the Incarnate God, Jesus. The divine dance is rhythmic and cyclical. Dissolving any distinction between dancer and observer implicates all creation in this divine dance. Such a powerful image reflects the ongoing invitation to be in a state of greater wakefulness. The dance is ongoing, with no beginning or ending. That which can change, however, is us and our relationship to such consciousness.

Theologian and Episcopal priest Carter Heyward uses the term *mutual relation* to speak to the nature of God and how Christians are called to be in this world. Heyward's reflections on the Trinity reiterate this sense of possibility and expansion. Perichoresis challenges us to leave behind our human desire for the predictable. Instead, we are called to broaden and refine our religious imagination. As Heyward argues, "God as Trinity means that whatever is Sacred is relational, never self-absorbed; always moving beyond itself to meet the new, the other, the different, never set in its ways or stuck on itself as the only way."[8] The interplay between sameness and difference, unity and multiplicity, is magnified in Heyward's words as she shifts the gaze outward into the space between and beyond. It's not just about us but about being part of something much larger. Movement, specifically movement toward difference in the spirit of relationality, is the essence of Trinitarian living. Moreover, she is keen to address stagnation as sin. Holding on to one way of being is rejecting the dynamism of the Trinity and thus turning away from God. For Heyward, innovation guided by mutual relation is itself holiness and wholeness. It's about facing outward and honoring the diversity and movement in our midst.

SIGNPOST TRINITY

In her landmark text *God for Us*, LaCugna breathes life into the history and theology of the doctrine of the Trinity. She looks deeply at the practical applications of this theology for faithful Christian living. She acknowledges the way the Trinity has been locked away as an abstraction, far from the reach of everyday baptized folks. Her work is an act of reorientation and resurrection. She writes, "The doctrine of the Trinity is not a theory about the essence of God conceived apart from the actual self-giving of God in the economy of salvation, but the essence of God revealed and bestowed in the person of Christ and in the permanent presence of the Spirit."[9] In this single sentence, LaCugna invites us to shake off the old and unrelatable reading of the Trinity and to enter into a physical and personal experience of the holy. She rejects the layers of translation and distance that come with conceiving the Trinity as simply the theory of the essence of God and grounds it instead in action. It is the essence revealed and bestowed. LaCugna empowers the baptized to draw upon their lives, Christ in their lives, the Spirit in their lives, to break open the mystery of God. She likens the Trinity to a signpost.[10] Like any signpost, the Trinity points beyond itself to reveal a path, a way. This image starkly contrasts with how the doctrine of the Trinity has been employed as a gatekeeper. Far from locking folks away or scaring them with imposing posturing, LaCugna's "Signpost Trinity" is a tool within the landscape. Even with all the incomprehensibility, the sign remains, pointing "beyond itself to the mystery of God who is alive and whose ongoing relationship with creation and persons cannot be frozen or fixed in time."[11] We may not understand it, but we feel it; we experience it in our bodies and the movement and relationships of our lives. Like a lighthouse, the signpost provides an orientation—it is in our midst whether we choose (or are able) to observe this reality. Whether we adjust accordingly or create the conditions to see more clearly is another question entirely.

RELATIONALITY

In an article published just a year after *God for Us*, LaCugna emphasizes this spirit of accessibility and authenticity. She writes,

> The central theme of all trinitarian theology is relationship: God's relationship with us, our relationship with one another. The doctrine of the Trinity is not an abstract conceptual paradox about God's inner life, or a mathematical puzzle of the "one in three." The doctrine of the Trinity is in fact the most

practical of all doctrines. Among other things, it helps us articulate our understanding of the gospel's demands: how personal conversion is related to social transformation; what constitutes "right relationship" within the Christian community and in society at large.[12]

LaCugna's bold insistence that the Trinity is "the most practical of all doctrines" deserves our attention. It is an invitation to see how our day-to-day lives may help elucidate the Trinitarian dynamism surrounding us, but it is also a challenge. What does it mean to bring the doctrine of the Trinity into our lives and to allow it to shape our days? On one level, we are already doing this work as we cross ourselves, but if we are to heighten our consciousness of what it means to mark our bodies with God's relationality, we may find more entry points for engaging meaningfully with this doctrine. There are real-life, on-the-ground social implications for embracing the Trinity's ongoing co-creative, self-giving, radically interdependent nature. One way of building this signpost into our lives is by reflecting theologically on moments of connection already unfolding in our living. These sites of wisdom offer us a deeply personal and relatable way of visualizing the shape of God's grace. We may even experience physiological changes as we recall those encounters of wonder and awe. Sometimes, the richest tidbits come when we least expect them.

The Gift of Revelation

I first met Michael when he visited campus as a prospective student. He and his family extended their visit to attend our 10 p.m. Mass. His parents and younger siblings sent him forth in August with excitement and trepidation. A profoundly engaged young man in his Catholic faith and an accomplished student in the School of Engineering, Michael sometimes struggled to connect socially with other students. Each Wednesday, he would come to the chapel at 5 p.m., make a cup of tea, and we would chat about our weeks. I got to know

Michael during these inventory sessions. I learned about his love of tabletop gaming and his baking prowess. He was a gardener back home and was elated to learn that fellow green thumbs on campus had started a community garden club.

One Friday night, at a Lenten simple supper, a group of us gathered at the Interfaith Center. We were seated at a long table in the downstairs meeting room, bodies squeezed shoulder to shoulder. As it turned out, Michael was the only male student present that night. I was conscious that all of these factors might make Michael uncomfortable. My worries, however, were quickly assuaged. He sat beside me and immediately took my infant son out of my arms, bouncing the baby on his knee. The women seated around us cooed and smiled, but Michael outshined everyone as the baby whisperer. He was a pro. As the oldest child in a large family, of course he was! I had never seen him smile so continuously. His eyes brightened, and his shoulders softened. It was magical the way Michael's uneasiness melted away. This young man, who I knew made conscious daily efforts to make eye contact and engage with others, was locking eyes with my son, making silly faces, and laughing with delight. It was a sacramental moment. I witnessed a deep and holy connectedness in that instant—bursting with joy and the spontaneous beauty they created together. God revealed an ever-presence in the divine dance between them and around us. Luckily, I was awake enough to catch a glimpse.

This moment was a revelation and transformation, not of Michael, of course, but of me and my perception of possibility. God's grace flowed through Michael's loving arms and full heart. God's grace poured through the unscripted silly ditties he made up on the spot and sang for my son. In that interaction, I could better see the image and likeness of God in Michael's *imago Dei* as he witnessed to the *imago Dei* of my son. That space between us was a gift of surprise, abundance, and tenderness. It was a reminder that there is always so much more than we can fathom—our God of abundance. We are called to be in relationship. As with this everyday moment after a long week, something profound happens when we are connected—and if we are oriented toward the sacred, we may even see God revealing the divine self in ordinary moments of connection like this one.

LaCugna argues that adoration is the "only appropriate response to the mystery of God revealed in the economy."[13] I love this insight. It reminds me that in the moment, I was awash with the spontaneity and beauty, and then I took a photo of them—Michael holding my son and the two of them beaming with the kind of smiles that transform the whole face. This was the only photo I took of the gathering that night, and I return to it now and then. Each time, I am moved to tears, met again with the revelation—the beauty and authenticity of these two people I love. Though this medium of technology might be a kind of translation, I am afforded a sacramental encounter of my own, an opportunity for adoration.[14] If we are to embrace the Trinity as a mystery of inclusion—unfolding around us, ready to be adored—how might we reorient ourselves to make room for all that beholding? How might spiritual practice and sacramental consciousness help make such adoration possible? And how might being in relationship—intentional, joy-filled, gritty relationship with people who are different from us—be a means by which to adore or behold the holiness of difference, dwelling in *imago Dei, imago Christi, imago Spiritus*?

The Call to Be in Relationship

The call to be in relationship, and to be in relationship with those who are different from us, is found throughout the New Testament. It also surfaces in official Church documents. When I began as a campus minister, this was news to me! I had been engaged in interfaith collaboration for years before I learned about this part of our history and the Church's commitment to encouraging interfaith dialogue. I had no idea that the baptized are called to be in relationship with people from other traditions. It was my friend in rabbinical school who taught me about *Nostra Aetate*, the document from the Second Vatican Council that redefined the Church's relationship to the Jewish community as well as folks from other traditions. While embarrassed to be in the dark about such important history, delight and affirmation quickly eclipsed those feelings of self-consciousness. It's no secret that people in the pews are often unaware of the richness of the tradition. Catholic Social Teaching (CST) continues to be virtually unknown. The only Tufts students I have encountered who have heard of CST are those who attended Catholic high schools. Sadly, many pastoral leaders can fail in their formation of Catholics by not teaching about these aspects of the tradition. This is a multidimensional, systemic issue, but two meaningful threads I see are limitations around capacity/resources and a culture of clericalism that, despite our best efforts, continues to infantilize laity—explicitly or implicitly. Despite more laypeople studying theology, there remains an enormous gap between the richness of our tradition and accessible opportunities to tap into that well for substantive growth. The writings of the Church are but a single example of an untapped resource standing right in our midst.

Conciliar and Postconciliar Documents

In this next section, I explore three Church documents that have significantly defined the Catholic Church's approach to relationships with religious others. Many scholars have devoted their lives to studying these documents and are deep within the weeds. This is not my training. I am a practitioner who finds inspiration in these documents and wishes to share them here with you. In my experience, the baptized are often unaware of the richness of these texts and might even consider them inaccessible. It is a loss that everyday Catholics are so distanced from the heart of these texts. For one, they are beautifully written. Poetic and profound, they unpack tradition and theology in ways that feel fresh and deeply connected to our shared history and legacy. While it is not a style of writing I would gravitate toward every day, I think we miss a great opportunity when Catholics are detached from this aspect of our tradition. In my brief outline here, I hope to provide an entry point for layfolk and to celebrate the beautiful ways our Church has called us to be in deep meaningful relationship with religious others.

The Declaration on the Relation of the Church to Non-Christian Religions: Nostra Aetate *(In Our Time)* was a 1964 landmark text from Vatican II. This proclamation was a direct response to the Second World War and the devastating loss of human life in the Holocaust. The second document is lesser known but a wonderfully rich follow-up written in 1984, *The Attitude of the Church toward Followers of Other Religions: Reflections and Orientations on Dialogue and Mission* (known colloquially as *Dialogue and Mission*). This text attempted to offer a practical application of *Nostra Aetate*. The third is from the Pontifical Council for Interreligious Dialogue (formerly Secretariat for Non-Christians, renamed in 1988), *Dialogue and Proclamation: Reflection and Orientations on Interreligious Dialogue and the Proclamation of the Gospel of Jesus Christ*, 1994. This final document, known colloquially as *Dialogue and Proclamation*, acknowledges the challenging work of honoring the call to evangelize while being conscientious, respectful agents within interfaith settings, where proselytizing is never the goal.

While these are the primary texts I will explore in this chapter, I reference two others that also contribute to the broader lens of interfaith dialogue, namely: *Dignitas Humanae* (Declaration of Religious Freedom, 1965) and *Gaudium et Spes* (Pastoral Constitution on the Church in the Modern World, 1965). Of course, the best way to appreciate these texts is to read them yourself, but I realize that it may be outside one's comfort zone, capacity, or simply not in the cards. While they are far more accessible than one might think, I take time here to lift up elements and sections that speak to this project. What follows is not a comprehensive deep dive into these texts but a peek into their beauty and richness, especially for those new to conciliar and postconciliar documents.

When *Nostra Aetate* (NA) was promulgated in 1964, the church officially redefined its relationship to other religious and philosophical traditions, with particular attention given to Judaism and the

Jewish people. Quite quickly, this conciliar document had a profound impact on the approach of Catholics toward religious others. Italian theologian Roberto Catalano uses the phrase "a new attitude" when discussing NA.[15] In this way, it was not a theological argument but a new posture or way of being in the world that *Nostra Aetate* called forth. Early in the text, we are met with the heart of the matter:

> The Church, therefore, exhorts her sons, that through dialogue and collaboration with the followers of other religions, carried out with prudence and love and in witness to the Christian faith and life, they recognize, preserve and promote the good things, spiritual and moral, as well as the socio-cultural values found among these men. (NA 2)

The urgency within this passage shakes me awake. Cross-worldview connections are not a casual recommendation, something to put at the end of a laundry list that you may or may not get to. No, we are exhorted—emphatically encouraged, urged, pressed—to reach out beyond the walls of our sanctuaries and liturgies to be with others. It is not ancillary to our identity as Catholics. Instead, it is central. It is a spiritual priority—something we are counseled to take on in life with fierce love and compassion. As this passage illuminates, we honor our faith and life when we "preserve and promote the good things" within other cultures and worldviews.

In the closing words of the text, these threads are woven together to reveal the fabric of the human family:

> We cannot truly call on God, the Father of all, if we refuse to treat in a brotherly way any man, created as he is in the image of God. Man's relation to God the Father and his relation to men his brothers are so linked together that Scripture says: "He who does not love does not know God" (1 John 4:8). No foundation therefore remains for any theory or practice that leads to discrimination between man and man or people and people, so far as their human dignity and the rights flowing

from it are concerned. The Church reproves, as foreign to the mind of Christ, any discrimination against men or harassment of them because of their race, color, condition of life, or religion. (NA, 5)

When I place these passages in conversation with one another, I am left with a deep sense of inspiration and direction. This work is urgent and requires empathy, compassion, and a heart longing for justice. The phrase "the mind of Christ" illuminates a way forward, referencing Philippians 2:5—a call to embrace Christ's humility. This is a source of clarity, of call—something I return to in my life and ministry. How do I cultivate humility as a way of being in the world? What actions in the everyday magnify Christ and his light? And how do we turn our hearts toward his radical love ethic—in the ordinary, unspectacular, yet wholly sacramental moments of life?

While *Nostra Aetate* was the primary text devoted to the church's relationship to other religious traditions, many Vatican II documents charted new paths regarding the religious other. For instance, *Gaudium et Spes (Pastoral Constitution on the Church in the Modern World*, 1965) begins by strengthening the deep connectedness between the Church and humanity. There is a real vision for redefining these relationships in the modern world: "Respect and love ought to be extended also to those who think or act differently than we do in social, political and even religious matters. In fact, the more deeply we come to understand their ways of thinking through such courtesy and love, the more easily will we be able to enter into dialogue with them" (GS 28). It is so powerful to see the roots of dialogue—honoring human dignity, postponing judgment, and trusting the Holy Spirit. We are called to befriend those who are different from us, those who have been pushed aside, misunderstood, or demonized.

Twenty years after Vatican II, the pastoral reflection *Dialogue and Mission* (1984) offered a practical application to the vision of *Nostra Aetate*. *Dialogue and Mission* (DM) sought to address the question: What does the spirit of *Nostra Aetate* look like in real life? While it is not a step-by-step handbook per se, the text maps out a more integrated and on-the-ground framework for developing meaningful relationships with followers of other traditions (DM 7).[16] A value that surfaces throughout is this emphasis on creating the conditions for "mutual understanding and enrichment" (DM 3) as well as respecting others in all their complexity. Moreover, DM is keen to bring interfaith dialogue to the forefront as a spiritual priority, meaning it is part of the Church's mission. Within certain circles, mission work is thought of solely through the lens of proselytization. This narrow and inaccurate understanding of the term does not capture the spirit of this text and, of course, is entirely inappropriate within interfaith contexts. Within DM, mission is presented as a "unified and complex reality." It is "living witness to Christian life," but must never be a justification for bludgeoning religious others. Drawing from the wisdom of another Vatican II document, *Dignitas Humanae* (Declaration of Religious Freedom), DM honors what I see as the two hands of mission: magnifying Christ's light in our thoughts, words, and deeds while also holding with deep care the "need to promote and respect the true freedom of the other person, rejecting any form of coercion whatsoever, especially in the religious sphere" (DM 18).

One of DM's powerful and poetic elements is the outline of different kinds of dialogue—Dialogue of Life, Dialogue of Action, Dialogue of Experts (or Theological Exchange), and Dialogue of Religious Experience. This document is extraordinary because it marks the first time the Catholic Church provided a classification or framework for dialogue.[17] As I read this section of DM for the first time, I came alive. The word *posture* kept coming back to me. How do we hold our bodies and spirits so as to foster dialogical existence—that is, a way of being in conversation with God and one another? The etymology of *dialogue* offers us a way in as well. In Greek, *dia* means *through*, and *logos* means *word* or *meaning*. The roots remind us that dialogue is dynamic, meaning *happening in movement*. I am reminded of the Holy Trinity and the kind of interplay between the three persons—the dance, as Richard Rohr would call it. DM captures this embodied and deeply mystical aspect of dialogue. In the Dialogue of Life, we see that "before all else, dialogue is a manner of acting, an attitude; a spirit which guides one's conduct. It implies concern, respect, and hospitality toward the other. It leaves room for the other person's identity, modes of expression and values.... Every follower of Christ, by reason of his human and Christian vocation, is called to live dialogue in his daily life" (DM 29, 30). There is a spaciousness and a graciousness in these words. I hear compassion and nonjudgment. I hear a call to adore the sacramental moments in our everyday lives. Those unspectacular encounters with human beings in the grocery store or on the sidewalk—they matter! That is cruciform living, staying awake to the points of intersection. As Sister Joan Chittister affirms in her reflection on Ordinary Time, "It is the daily—the way we act ordinarily, not rarely that defines us as either kind, or angry, or faithful, or constant."[18] Are we closed off to God's ever-present invitation to be in communion with creation? Or do we bring a dialogical spirit, a hospitable heart, with us on our daily journey?

While the three other forms of dialogue are powerful witnesses to this ethic, they each flow from the life source that is this original posture. Nevertheless, I briefly map them out here to lift up what I see as the heart of DM. The Dialogue of Action calls us to prioritize working together for human liberation and the work of justice. The Dialogue of Theological Exchange centers the value of leaders going deep, engaging expertise to build something beautiful together—addressing a shared issue or seeking to grow in understanding. The fourth form, the Dialogue of Religious Experience, lifts up the transformative power of sharing ritual, prayer, contemplation, and action across tradition. Of course, this form requires special attention, care, reverence, and humility. In chapters 5 and 6, I unpack this theme of humility, especially as it pertains to Christians operating responsibility and conscientiously in multifaith spaces.

When I began reading these postconciliar texts several years ago, I was so moved by the language. A passage in *Proclamation and Dialogue* (1994) was particularly clarifying: "Interreligious dialogue does not merely aim at mutual understanding and friendly relations. It reaches a much deeper level, that of the spirit, where exchange and sharing consists in a mutual witness to one's beliefs and a common exploration of one's respective religious convictions. In dialogue, Christians and others are invited to deepen their religious commitment, to respond with increasing sincerity to God's personal call and gracious self-gift" (DP 40). It is heartening to see such deep value and reverence for co-creativity. Just look at this terminology: *mutual witness*, *common exploration*, *religious commitment*, *sincerity*, *personal call*, *gracious self-gift*. When we commune together in dialogue, we get beneath the surface. We may begin with our commonalities, that is *just* the beginning. Moving at the speed of trust, we are able to hold our differences with deep care and create something new and something beautiful. It is a faithful process that requires deep listening and honestly seeing one another, themes that we will explore in the next chapter. I want to note that these moments are often beyond language—pointing toward the ineffable. In our approximations with language, we are met with limitations, but it is often worth the attempt to convey and better understand the experience. I will close this chapter with one such attempt—a story that embodies the fourth type of dialogue, the Dialogue of Religious Experience.

Dialogue of Religious Experience

In April 2021, I wept as I watched Holy Thursday services on a screen from the study in our bungalow. I longed for the embodied worship experience, always my favorite liturgy of the year. I longed to hold the heel of a stranger in my hand, massaging their arch with tenderness. I longed to see the stewards in the sanctuary holding towels and bowls, guiding the congregation through the upper room ritual. I thought of the people in the past who had washed my feet. The arthritic man at the monastery who carefully knelt before me, his knobbed knuckles pouring warm water out of a carafe. Kate, a Lutheran classmate of mine from Harvard Divinity School, brought me to my first proper foot-washing liturgy. And, of course, my friend Heather, who loves Holy Thursday and often talks about "bringing our lives to the basin to do a little scrubbing." But there I was that night, alone, strangely living my tradition that felt at once near and far.

When I imagined what it would be like to return to in-person worship after the Covid-19 lockdown, I could hardly bear it. Like a teenager fantasizing about romantic love, I was overcome by a flood of emotions and a sense of looming possibility. My body tasted that sense of release and wonder. My chest heaved, and tears streamed down my cheeks. It was intense and profound, and it was unclear whether my body could hold all I was experiencing. I pictured myself standing at the front of Goddard Chapel, weeping as I tried to address our congregation of students and neighbors. That image made me wonder if I should get it out of my system before returning to work that fall. (You know, for the sake of professionalism!) But then I decided this was one of those moments of pastoral vulnerability that could be a doorway for others.

After all those dreamings, my first in-person worship after the lockdown didn't occur in a parish or in Goddard Chapel. It was at Tufts Hillel for a Shabbat service. It was the beginning of the academic year in the fall of 2021. We had just started welcoming students to campus in staggered waves—with local folks arriving last. As I entered the building, I was filled with trepidation. "Should we be doing this?" I wondered. Though I have been crossing that threshold for over fifteen years (first as a student at Tufts and then as a staff member in the University Chaplaincy), it felt like a whole new world. There we were—students, faculty, and staff—emerging from that strange liminal space of the past year and a half.

Every student present that night had just endured the elaborate testing protocol and isolation process required for move-in. Many were new to campus, beginning their college experience amid pandemic restrictions and risk. Others were returners grateful to be back even with the limitations of the moment. I walked into the familiar upstairs sanctuary and could tell from his eyes that my colleague, the rabbi, was smiling. Always a student-led service, the leaders were spread throughout the circle of chairs. Outside of my immediate family, this was the closest I had been to other people in a year and a half. Despite being early evening and still light outside, the brightness of our masks caught my eye in the window's reflection—a new era had begun.

Like everyone else, I followed the Shabbat leader's instructions and turned to the page for the first song. The other service leaders began singing, and though they sang the same words, it was quickly apparent that they were singing different tunes. In the chaos of traveling to campus, dealing with protocols limiting social contact, and the challenge of simply being a human in the pandemic, they had not been able to prepare as they usually would have. Right then and there, in the middle of the service, the leaders shared aloud the tunes each of them knew for these prayers. One person would start singing, and then a few folks would chime in. "I know that tune from camp," one said. "Me too," said another. If enough folks knew the tune, the song would take off, the assembly following along and learning as we went.

I was in awe of these students. There they were cocreating this service together—in real time! The symbolism of finding a common tune was almost too much. I laughed inside, delighted by it all, swaying and stomping my feet with the congregation. As is usually my experience in Shabbat service, I was inspired by all the singing. It's not just the leaders or experienced choristers. No. At our Shabbat services, everyone sings; you can feel it transform the space between us. That night, our voices filled the small sanctuary, and I remembered what it was like to create something beautiful, spontaneously beautiful, with other human beings. I remembered what it was like to experience joyful noise—completely enchanted by the observance of these young people building something new . . . again. When we eventually spilled outside to eat Shabbat dinner under an enormous tent in the parking lot, I came into consciousness of my revelry. Had I just been singing and praying in a room full of people? Yes. Yes, I had.

That evening—in all its gritty, organic, poetic beauty—turned out to also be a harbinger of the challenges we would face in chaplaincy and beyond. Learning to be community mid/post-pandemic has taken time. It has been beautiful, and it has been messy. It is still beautiful and still messy. It remains, however, a gift and something

I hope I never again take for granted. In sharing that holy space with our Jewish friends, I was reminded of one of my favorite sources of deep comfort: We never have to do it alone. From my tradition, I would say the Spirit moves. The Spirit guides us. The Spirit guided me to that gathering that warm summer night. After so many months in lockdown, I needed deep spiritual renewal. I needed to be reminded of the joy of shared space and the depth of possibility when we trust the winding path of spiritual journey.

Spiritual Provocation: Interbeing

Sometimes, we need reminders that we are not alone and are part of something larger. And sometimes those reminders are right beside us… or in our pockets! The first time we ran our interfaith friendship program at Tufts University was in the fall of 2020. The challenges and limitations of the moment were great. The needs in our community here were high and so was that sense of apartness. In this context, our new offering felt all the more vital. Each of our chaplains wrote spiritual practices that we gave to our participant dyads. My friend and then-colleague, Buddhist Chaplain Priya wrote a practice I loved! Over time, we have adapted this exercise for various settings, but the heart of it remains the same: a powerful passage from beloved Vietnamese teacher and leader Thích Nhất Hạnh. He was a Zen master and civil rights activist who inspired and guided millions of human beings from around the globe. His home, Plum Village in France, continues to be a site for pilgrimage and learning even after his passing in 2022.

When contemplating the nature of our interdependent existence, Thích Nhất Hạnh reflected on language and how to communicate this element of our lives together on this planet. He explained:

> About thirty years ago I was looking for an English word to describe our deep interconnection with everything else. I liked the word "togetherness," but I finally came up with the word "interbeing." The verb "to be" can be misleading, because we

cannot be by ourselves, alone. "To be" is always to "inter-be." If we combine the prefix "inter" with the verb "to be," we have a new verb, "inter-be." To inter-be and the action of interbeing reflects reality more accurately. We inter-are with one another and with all life.[19]

I invite you to take a moment and reread this passage. Allow the words to hang in the air around you. Take a few deep breaths. Breathe in. Pause. Breathe out. Pause. Let the words settle deep into your body.

Now, turn to your phone or photograph album and find a photo that somehow captures this insight from Thích Nhất Hạnh. Choose an image from your life that communicates the reality of our interconnectedness or inter-being with others and the natural world. It could be a photo from a recent trip where you were surprised by all you had in common with the strangers you met, or of a garden, a beloved, or a funny sign you saw on the sidewalk that reminded you of a friend who lives on the other side of the world. It could be a picture of a family member you miss deeply who has recently passed or a silly photo of your feet, which transports you to being an eight-year-old and realizing they look just like your uncle's. The point is to orient yourself toward the interconnection and inter-being around you. Become aware of how you are already oriented toward that sense of belonging. You did, after all, take that photo.

Questions to ponder:

What was speaking to you then, and what prompted you to capture it?
Who or what is at the center, and what ripple effects of impact or influence do you see?
How does your photo communicate inter-being?
What observation or insight might you take into your day from this photo and exercise?

CHAPTER THREE

Listening to God, Ourselves, and One Another

My spouse Andrew and I met in the local storytelling community in Cambridge. One night, he told a great story about being a chaplain in the hospital ICU, and I went up to speak to him during intermission. A few weeks later, we went on our first date at a story slam in Jamaica Plain, and we have been hanging out ever since. I loved volunteering with this community-based storytelling organization. I met incredible human beings like Andrew, but it also offered a window into human connection. My favorite job at those story slams was signing folks up to be one of the ten tellers for the evening. When I would approach people to see if they were interested in putting their name in the hat, guests would typically fall into one of three categories: the enthusiastic, often seasoned teller who had a story prepared and would be crestfallen if we didn't call their name; the on-the-fence teller who was new to the scene but brought their friends for moral support and encouragement; and the person who, when I walked up to the table to ask if anyone was thinking of telling a story, would look at me with horror and confusion.

"Me, tell a story?" they would gasp. "No way. I am just here to watch. You'll never find me behind a microphone."

While it wasn't a sure thing, over time I learned that this third group of people—those who balked at the idea of standing in front of a room of strangers and opening their hearts—often put their names in the hat before the night was through.

Something happens when we listen.

Listening transforms us. It opens doors—outside and inside. Folks in the audience at our events saw themselves in the tellers. Listening to others stirred something within them, and like Julie at the interfaith open mic, they said yes to an experience that seemed impossible in another setting or just a moment before. In this chapter, I will explore the transformational practice of listening—how it changes those who listen and how it changes those who are heard. First, I turn to our tradition and a single story within Scripture that offers insight into the spirituality of listening. I then lift up the practice of active listening to demystify and magnify these critical skills. Examples and exercises appear throughout the chapter so you work out your listening muscles and see how active listening can be incorporated into everyday life.

Tradition: Listening in Scripture with Lydia

If we ever forget that a bunch of human beings created our church, we should go back and reread the Acts of the Apostles. I love these gritty stories and how they often feature frustrations between friends and no single vision for what we would now call *church*. However, amid this messiness, their desire to listen to the Holy Spirit endures. These Jesus followers always try to keep their hearts turned toward God so God may lead them in the right direction. During Eastertide, when we read large sections of Acts in liturgy, we witness the dynamics of this early Jesus movement, and we may even see ourselves in their humanity. It is always important to remember that we are modern-day apostles, and even though we live with two thousand years of tradition, we are still finding our way.

The excerpt below is just a single story from Acts of the Apostles. It will guide us in this study of listening.

> We set sail from Troas and took a straight course to Samothrace, the following day to Neapolis, and from there to Philippi, which is a leading city of the district of Macedonia and a Roman colony. We remained in this city for some days. On the sabbath day we went outside the gate by the river, where we supposed there was a place of prayer; and we sat down and spoke to the women who had gathered there. A certain woman named Lydia, a worshipper of God, was listening to us; she was from the city of Thyatira and a dealer in purple cloth. The Lord opened her heart to listen eagerly to what was said by Paul. When she and her household were baptized, she urged us, saying, 'If you have judged me to be faithful to the Lord, come and stay at my home.' And she prevailed upon us.
> (Acts of the Apostles 16:11–15 NRSV)

This passage marks a turning point in both the narrative style of the Acts of the Apostles and growth within the early church. For the text itself, there is a distinct shift in the narrator's voice. Until this point, the adventures of the apostles spreading the gospel are all told in the third person. Acts begins with an affectionate salutation addressed to Theophilos (literally *God-lover* or *Friend of God*), and we as readers are regaled with tales of the apostles trying to figure out what their lives will be like now that Jesus is no longer with them on earth. In chapter 16, however, we are abruptly met with a collective narrator in the first-person plural.[1] The second significant detail within this passage is its depiction of the first Christian convert in Macedonia and, therefore, Europe.[2] Her name is Lydia. She is often referred to as a businesswoman or even framed as an entrepreneur. What we know of her is limited, but like so many moments within the text—and the text of our lives—there is much to mine beneath the surface. Lydia is from Thyatira, a city in modern-day Turkey, known to be a hub for the textile trade, especially for purple cloth.[3] While we do not know if she was selling her cloth at the river, we know that this is her industry. Purple was and still is a color associated with means and power. It signified a regal sensibility and high social positionality in antiquity, as the dyeing process was so involved and the final products exorbitantly expensive. These colors came from the ocean; mollusks were processed, pulverized, dried, and boiled.[4] It was a painstaking endeavor and one also reputed for the stench it left within the fabrics—not too surprising given the source of the dye! This is Lydia's world.

That day, however, she is at the river. Perhaps she is hanging out with the other women, chatting, catching up, and talking about the strange newcomers in town (i.e., the Jesus followers). Or perhaps she is separate from all of that, inhabiting a favorite perspective of the author of Acts—the outsider or onlooker. In whichever way we imagine the beginnings of this scene, it is in this context that she hears the testimony of the apostles and is forever changed. The text reads, "Lydia, a worshipper of God, was listening to us. . . . The Lord opened her heart to listen eagerly to what was said by Paul." I feel my posture shift when I pray with this short passage. My shoulders widen, my chest falls into exhale, my arms bend at the elbow, and my palms face outward. It's almost contagious, that God-opened heart of hers! Despite the two millennia between us, I see possibility and empathy pouring through her body. The word transforms her—her heart is malleable and agile. She brings home this good news, and as with many women in the early church, she leads her entire household to the baptismal waters. She is a woman of agency with financial independence and models a spirit of humility and surrender required of conversion.

Lydia's receptivity and generosity on the shores of the river manifest as hospitality. As the story ends, she opens her home to Paul and his entourage of misfits, insisting that they stay with her. Listening with a heart open for transformation, Lydia's world gets larger, not smaller. Her community and household face outward, toward service and communion. There is so much wisdom here as we think about our engagement with the everyday, unspectacular moments that define our lives.

Let's return to the beginning of this passage and imagine Paul and the apostles deciding to go for a walk to find a place for prayer on the Sabbath. Where did they go? They went where they "supposed there was a place of prayer." Think back to when you were visiting a new place and trying to explore. Maybe you were also looking for a place to pray or get a good cup of coffee or a meal. Were you standing on the sidewalk looking at a map or trying to catch the eye of a local walking by? What do those conversations sound like? How might your experience in a new place offer a way to contemplate the apostles in this scene and the spirit of spontaneity that brought them to the river?

Many of us live hyper-scheduled lives. We may assume there is no space for spontaneity, for the stroll to the river or the conversation with strangers. Our culture engages with time so differently now. This is true even if we think back ten or twenty years before the advent of smartphones. I see this change on campus, where cultural trends feel compressed and intensified. Students often plan out their days by intervals of a half hour or even fifteen minutes. For many, this kind of structure is a profound source of comfort and may even be a necessary adaptive strategy, given different learning styles and neurodivergence. It is important not to demonize but to contextualize. Does our relationship with technology help us to listen, or is it creating a barrier? Maybe it is both—depending on the situation and the time of day. When we look at Lydia's wisdom, however, we know something powerful happened that day at the river. Perhaps we might challenge ourselves to be open to the spontaneity of the Holy Spirit and experiment with unscripted moments. What inspiration do you find in the story of Lydia?

Synodality: The Listening Church

I have been inspired and energized by the three-year synodal process that Pope Francis opened in 2021. Synodality means *journeying together*. Pope Francis's vision for journeying together was rooted in bringing together layfolk, clergy, religious, and bishops to do the deep listening—listening to what is on the hearts of God's people and listening to the Holy Spirit. In many ways this is an ancient practice—there have been synods before—but the fact that laypeople and women religious are literally at the table with voting rights makes this synod something new. The process has taken shape through on-the-ground listening sessions in parish halls, schools, and other community settings. There is a deep vulnerability in synodality. It recognizes that the Holy Spirit continues to speak, and it is through intentionally listening to one another that we will better understand where God is calling us. It is about listening, discernment, and mission. What does it mean and look like to *be* church in the twenty-first century? Listening is transformative, and it is through listening and participation that we stay awake to the Holy Spirit moving in and between us. Pope Francis offered clarity and vision when he explained that "a synodal church is a listening church, knowing that listening 'is more than feeling.' It is a mutual listening in which everyone has something to learn. Faithful people, the College of Bishops, the Bishop of Rome: we are one in listening to others; and all are listening to the Holy Spirit, the 'Spirit of truth' (Jn 14:17), to know what the Spirit 'is saying to the Churches' (Rev 2:7)."[5]

Being in communion with one another, lifting up the gifts and wisdom of all, and pointing outward toward the world—this is how we come to know where God is calling us. This is the deep listening that is taking place within our parishes and communities right now. At times, it feels aspirational. The process has not been perfect, and yet seeing such a commitment to a new/old way of being church is heartening and affirming. Many have written extensively on the complexity of issues within the Synod on Synodality. While I cannot dive into the nuances of this critical work in this book, I celebrate the model that prioritizes listening, mission, and participation—necessary components to interfaith engagement as well.

Last year, on retreat, I led a practice of Visio Divina (divine seeing/gazing). Drawing from the ancient tradition of Lectio Divina (divine reading), which I explore more deeply in the next chapter, we used art instead of scripture, dwelling in the presence of God and creative expression, allowing the Spirit to speak to us. I laid thirty or so pieces of devotional artwork on the table. They spanned the globe—Christian artists from Nigeria, India, China, Japan, Cameroon, Brazil, Mexico, First Nations, and the United States. They were icons and biblical scenes, each so unique and contextually specific.

One image was a piece of digital art inspired by the Synod on Synodality, which was that gathering of bishops, religious, priests, and layfolk in Rome to unpack what was spoken, heard and learned in the listening sessions. The young woman who chose to pray with this artwork had never heard the word *synod*, but she was drawn to the image—people of different races and cultures sitting at the table together, their arms outstretched, almost deferring to, pointing toward the Holy Spirit. The image was framed by loaves and fishes and the scales of justice. As she reflected later, the bright colors and beautiful patterns also spoke to her. It was unexpected. That exercise helped her understand just how vital colors are to her spiritual life—a connection to her mother and grandmother. I share this anecdote because I continue to reflect on what it meant for someone to be so taken by the essence of synodality. As I mentioned, she was unfamiliar with the word, but she knew in her bones the practical and spiritual wisdom of orienting ourselves around one another—and around those who are different from us. Moreover, her theological reflection on the color insight demonstrated a deep reading of the moment. She listened to the Spirit speaking through the piece of artwork and she listened to that part of herself she hadn't yet fully understood. There was so much beneath the surface.

WHAT ACTUALLY HAPPENS WHEN WE LISTEN?

One night, when Andrew and I were hosting a story slam in downtown Boston, I approached a woman who had just sat at her table. I asked my question in a cheerful tone: "Are you thinking of telling a story tonight?" She had no idea what I was talking about. She had just entered the restaurant for dinner and was seated in the upper room where we were preparing for the story slam. When I explained what would happen in the space that night, she was excited but insisted that she was not interested in sharing. English was not her first language, she explained. She had been in town visiting her son briefly and was getting ready for an early flight the following day. Midway through the evening, however, this audience member approached me and put her name in the hat. Shortly after, we pulled her name, and she reluctantly came to the stage and told a story about literal border crossing. First, she made us cry with a narrative of heartache, and by the end, the whole room was howling with laughter. I wondered how often she had told this story in her native tongue—recounting the moment she and her family, packed in the car, realized that her spouse had misspoken to a border patrol agent. Instead of extending a greeting, he had accidentally offered a salacious non sequitur. The assembly loved it, and she won the slam that night.

The backroom evenings and basement stages where we hosted storytelling nights became living, breathing sanctuaries as strangers held the stories of others with genuine care. Our evenings together were steeped in co-creative energies. It was a deeply supportive environment, so the audience would cheer them on even if someone got up to the stage and found themselves unnerved or too anxious to proceed. I welcomed this beautiful reminder that we are just a bunch of human beings coming together to be real. I used to joke that "this is what churches think they do." Having also attended twelve-step meetings, I can confidently say those meetings are an even better model for churches. In the rooms, we make space for individuals to share their stories and learn from one another. Folks are affirmed and transformed by the reality that we are not so unique—our suffering and joy are like that of so many human beings, those still living and those who have gone before us.

Carl Rogers and Active Listening

In the mid-twentieth century, the esteemed psychologist Carl Rogers created the client-centered approach, which is the basis of many talk therapy modalities today. It was revolutionary because of its emphasis on empathy, trust building, and the clinician's unconditional positive regard for their client. Rogers observed that clients were more likely to develop self-awareness, grow in self-worth, and address their challenges if they felt supported, affirmed, and accompanied. Central to the client-centered approach is active listening. The clinician might ask clarifying questions, but their role is that of a listener.

Rogers and his partner Richard Farson lift up the multidirectional nature of active listening—it allows those speaking and sharing to feel seen and heard. Still, it also changes the interior landscape of the listener.[6] This two-way street of active listening creates the conditions for transformation. They write, "When people are listened to sensitively, they tend to listen to themselves with more care and to make clear exactly what they are feeling and thinking. Group members tend to listen more to each other, to become less argumentative, more ready to incorporate other points of view. Because listening reduces the threat of having one's ideas criticized, the person is better able to see them for what they are and is more likely to feel that his contributions are worthwhile. Not the least important result of listening is the change that takes place within the listener himself."[7]

This passage is an invitation to a different orientation. Listening, as they claim, is contagious. If I train myself to listen with respect and care to others, I am more likely to turn that intentionality back onto myself. It is within these contexts that we learn about our biases and discomforts. At which point in the story did I bristle? Did something surprise me or challenge me? In professional ministry formation, we ask the question: when did I leave the room? In other words, when did I internally react in a way that caused me to lose focus and center my needs instead of remaining present? I am not a failure if I leave the room, but doing so reveals that more work must be done to better understand my inner landscape.

Each year, I teach students about active listening. Drawing from the rich well of resources in this field, I focus on three foundational elements:

Just be present

The central component of active listening is being present. This means not thinking about what you will say next. It is natural for our minds to wander and connect what someone is saying to our own experience. In active listening, we do not interrupt to say, "that reminds me of the time…." Rather, we receive their sharing as a gift. This can be hard at first. But I promise you that with practice, you will be able to flex that muscle just like you would if you were putting in the hours at the gym.

Nonverbal connection

The goal is to communicate to your partner *I am with you*. Think of how your body posture and facial expressions give that validation. You are not to interrupt your partner, but there might be small expressions such as *hmm* or *wow* that will convey your attentiveness. Are you concentrating so hard on not thinking about what you will say next that your brows are furrowed and your neck tense? Are you slouching in your chair with your arms crossed, or are you sitting upright, open-chested, with your shoulders at ease? There are many ways that we communicate to our storyteller that we are listening.

Silence

Fear not! Silence is okay; more often than not, silence is pregnant with all sorts of richness. This exercise will give you practice in getting comfortable with silence in everyday life. If you can model ease with silence or even with a slight lull in conversation, it will allow your partner an opportunity to breathe and not feel rushed to speak. Experiment with sitting in silence by yourself. Periodic silence sessions of five to ten minutes will help build resilience and familiarity with the practice. (I explain this more in the coming sections.) In our overstimulating culture, embracing silence can feel radical and awkward. Be patient with yourself and remember that all of this work is connected.

PRACTICE: ACTIVE LISTENING

I invite you to contact a friend or family member and experiment with active listening yourself! If you would like a road map, feel free to follow the steps below.

Step 1: Reflection

Both you and your partner should take time to reflect for five to ten minutes. You may journal or go for a walk with the following prompt: Tell a story about a time when you have experienced of wonder. It could be a recent memory or something from your childhood. Take time to put yourself back in that place. Remember what makes a good story—details. Engage your senses—what does it sound like in that moment? What does it look like, feel, taste, and smell like? Once you have your story and are ready, check in with your partner.

Step 2: Storytelling and Story Receiving

Allow three minutes for the first person to tell their story. Make sure to set a timer.

Step 3: Reflecting Back

After this person finishes, the listener will return the story to the teller. You can paraphrase and use the same language. Just do your best to capture that experience of wonder.

Step 4: Giving Feedback

The original teller will then offer feedback. Did your partner capture your story accurately? If there are details that need clarifying or adjusting, please provide that information.

Step 5: Incorporating Feedback

The listener tells the story again but incorporates the original teller's feedback.

Step 6: Switch Places

Change places. Have the listener become the storyteller, and repeat the process.

Step 7

Once you have both told your stories of wonder and gone through the listener feedback process, take a moment to reflect on these questions:

- What was it like to be the storyteller and listener?
- What was hard, and what came easy?
- Did anything surprise you?
- What was it like to have your story told back to you?
- How might you bring a posture of wonder to the practice of active listening?

LISTENING TO THE WORLD AROUND US, LISTENING TO GOD

I find the early hours of the morning enchanting. Something about that liminal time of day offers me clarity and a deep sense of connectedness. When our windows are open in the spring and summer, I lay in bed listening to the birdsong filling our residential city neighborhood. They begin at three o'clock in the morning, their music meandering through our house, making it hard to distinguish between the world outside and inside the home. In those moments, I sense the presence of Saint Brigid. Being raised Irish Catholic, I saw the cross of Saint Brigid everywhere as a kid, but it wasn't until I met my dear friend Chris that I had a chance to sit with Brigid's story. As I mentioned in chapter 1, Brigid of Kildare was born neither an enslaved person nor free, neither indoors nor outdoors, neither day nor night, neither pagan nor Christian, neither winter nor spring. She is our liminal saint, a woman who embodied hybridity, margins, and thresholds. She is Our Lady of the Thin Places.

The birdsong hour is the hour of Saint Brigid. During this time, I am flooded with a sense of peace, spaciousness, and clear-headedness that are increasingly less accessible as the day goes on. Saint Brigid calls me into the silence—which is ultimately not too silent at all! It is layered with a chorus of birds and our dog's paws tapping against the hardwood floor as she moseys around the house, checking in on us and looking for a different place to sleep. It is layered with the sounds of squirrels knocking over planters in our garden as they furiously dig for seeds and with the garbage truck crash every Tuesday morning. Contemplatives invite us to try on silence and listening. I encourage you to experiment with it yourself. Start small. Sit in silence for five minutes and then for ten. Set a timer and allow yourself to stay awake to all that unfolds—the noises inside your head and outside in the world. Listening is about bringing awareness to the moment, not white-knuckling each second and resisting noise, but being open and witnessing it. Each time you stray or get caught up in a stream of thought, invite yourself (in a nonjudgmental way) to return to the silence. Do not get upset if you keep getting distracted. Distractions are natural and part of the cognitive process. Everyone experiences distractions. Attentiveness to silence is a practice that requires a set of muscles that only develop if we work them out. Getting impatient with ourselves will only take us further out of the moment. Buddhist friends and meditation teachers have taught me over the years to wave hello to these thoughts, acknowledge their presence, and let them float by. Then, recenter. After a session, however, I recommend bringing a spirit of curiosity and wonder to the practice. Perhaps there is a reason why you stray at a particular moment each time in the exercise. Is there a pattern?

Theologian and writer Kevin O'Brien brings another lens to this theme of distraction. In his book *The Ignatian Adventure*, O'Brien notes that "what at first seems like a distraction offers an opportunity for a graced encounter with God. Thus, if the distracting thought continues, carefully discern whether it's a distraction or something you need to pray about."[8] O'Brien's words call us to trust—trust in God, trust in ourselves, and trust in the long-view of prayer. It is not all about instant answers or a conscious understanding of our prayer life. God is always working beneath the surface, often out of sight and out of reach. When we trust in the potter (God), we allow ourselves (the clay) to be formed along the way. Freeing ourselves from a transactional relationship to time and "productivity" takes patience and discipline. If we can trust in God, we can allow ourselves the spaciousness to just be with God and not extract every experience for benchmarks.

My friend Holly is a chaplain, and she often reminds her clients and students that spiritual practice doesn't always feel good. I love the realness in her words. It is not uncommon for us to put prayer or spiritual practice on a pedestal. We might be looking for perfect moments or transcendent experiences, but it might just be an average day. Spirituality is not unlike physical fitness in that way. We don't go to the gym expecting personal records every day. If we did, we would be at risk of injuring both our bodies and spirits! While there are fabulous workouts that are substantive and satisfying, more often than not, our legs feel heavy from not getting great sleep, or we are sluggish from having a late lunch during a busy workday. Nevertheless, when we leave, we know we have put in the work.

Lay Cistercian Carl McColman takes this one step further. In his reflection on contemplation, he explains that "God comes to you to be in relationship, not just to make you feel good. So contemplation ultimately nurtures you at a level far deeper than emotions or conscious awareness."[9] Throughout his writing, McColman calls his readers back to the reality of God's greatness, remarking on how very human it is to want to be in control. This short passage from his *Big Book of Christian Mysticism* is another way of communicating this truth. We human beings cannot always see God working. We are called, however, to trust in the process and to show up. Getting used to a different prayer and spiritual practice rubric may take time. That is okay. Our relationship with God evolves and matures as we go through life. We do not always do a good job of normalizing this process or offering opportunities for adult spiritual formation. However, it is okay to leave behind old images and practices that no longer serve you.

MONO-TASKING

As you may have gathered by now, I consider active listening akin to my fitness workouts—muscles requiring attention and training. It takes time, but anyone can develop these life-giving skills with care, patience, and persistence.

In our culture today, we have so many distractions. Our relationship with time can feel transactional between tight schedules, push notifications, and unrealistic expectations from the norm of over-programming. In this time-scarcity model, we are encouraged to multitask. Multitasking can make us feel efficient and effective, but often, it means doing several things poorly. MIT professor and researcher Sherry Turkle writes, "Multitasking gives us a neurochemical high, so we think we are doing better and better when actually we are doing worse and worse."[10] In her research, Turkle found that even though her students thought they could multitask at no cost to performance, they consistently underperformed in both activities.[11] When our attention is divided, we miss details and cannot get beneath the surface.

When we engage in active listening, we mono-task. We focus on the person before us and what they share—verbally and nonverbally. Through our focus and presence, we say *you are enough and worthy of our attention*. Again, this is a move away from a transactional culture and toward one of meaningful connection—I am not thinking about what I will do with this information or what I will say next. I am not thinking about what points I want to make, not thinking about parallels to my life or what to say to "win" an argument in the conversation. I am focused on listening to honor what has been shared as a living, breathing thing—that is the point of the entire exercise. It is within these conditions that empathy grows.

In his beautiful book *Befriending Silence*, Carl McColman offers this practical wisdom regarding silence and listening:

> You'll notice that this kind of gentle silent prayer may not feel "productive" or like it gets any "results." Good. We live in a world that has turned productivity into an idol. Maybe at the office productivity is king, but when it comes to our relationship with God, we need to learn to let go and simply be. Let God take the lead. Our job is not to tell God what to do, but to listen to God, and for God, with the ear of our heart. Finding time every day for silence helps us, in a wonderful way, to cultivate open-ended listening.[12]

Many of us need this reminder daily! I know I do. As a lover of audiobooks and podcasts, I must intentionally carve out time for silence. Our culture's rubrics around time and productivity do not translate to our relationship with God. It is hard to recalibrate when every other moment of life engages a different set of values. Breaking free of the multitask myth is part of this work. More is not inherently better. This sentiment is countercultural; know you are not alone if you find it challenging. Mindfulness is the opposite of multitasking and skimming the surface. It centers us down into a single action in the present moment.

SPIRITUAL PRACTICE: MINDFULNESS

Before Mass each Sunday at Goddard Chapel, I welcome our community by offering a short reflection question and inviting students

LISTENING TO GOD, OURSELVES, AND ONE ANOTHER

to turn to their neighbors to introduce themselves. Then, we move to a time of mindfulness meditation. Because it can be intimidating for some students to experiment with mindfulness meditation, I try to make it as approachable as possible. While I am sure not everyone is into it, I am constantly amazed by how genuinely students embrace this practice. Many close their eyes and keep them closed long after I finish. There have been times when our celebrant has been running late and these mindfulness sessions exceeds ten or even fifteen minutes. Such moments remind me of just how hungry they are—and perhaps we all are—to center down and just be. It can be hard to transition from the busyness of life to liturgy—and to the headspace and heart space we want and need to be fully present for Mass. It is better to name that spiritual challenge and provide a pathway than to ignore the elephant in the room.

Here is a short exercise you can try on your own. Feel free to adapt as you see fit. If you are new to meditation, you may record yourself slowly reading the passage below and then play it back as a guided meditation or just read along as you go, pausing after each sentence. Feel free to experiment to find what kind of entry point will be most effective for you as you try to stay awake to the present moment. For some, the phone will be a helpful tool; for others, its mere presence may sully the atmosphere. You do you in finding a pathway forward.

I invite you to do whatever you need to do to feel grounded. You may sit upright in a chair, lie down, or stand outside in your garden. You may choose to close your eyes or soften your gaze. Wherever you are, feel where your body meets the earth. Take a few deep breaths. Breathe in, pause, breathe out, pause. Slow your exhale, drawing it out as long as you can. In through your nose, out through your mouth. Feel the breath of life take up space within your body. Feel your belly rise and fall. As you breathe in, pause, breathe out, pause. Bring your awareness to this pause—the gift of rest and the invitation to just be resides within each breath you take throughout the day. When we breathe, we are changed—physiologically and spiritually—when we breathe together, we are the body of Christ. Now close this time with two more deep breaths. Amen.

CREATING A CONTAINER TO LISTEN

At the beginning of the lockdown, three of my colleagues and I formed a working group focused on spiritual care. We did a deep dive into the field's literature and interviewed students to learn how they thought of this part of our work within the University Chaplaincy. It was a great project amid pandemic uncertainty—offering meaningful touch points for students, faculty, and staff. When we sat with the data mid-summer, the term that came up most for students, the term they used to convey meaningful experiences with the chaplaincy, was *check-in*. At first, I questioned this phrase. Is that all we do? Is that how students think of spiritual care—just checking in?

However, I started to see it differently once I put myself in their shoes. It is always important to honor the words that others use, and when I did so in conversation with the reflections they offered, I saw such richness and wisdom. In the freneticism of their day-to-day lives on campus, the University Chaplaincy was where they felt they could be real. *Check-ins* may have had this casual sound because it *was* casual, spontaneous, and unscripted! The difference was that it was also spacious—and they felt meaningfully listened to. Students reported that they felt comfortable being authentic in these moments. They could share what was hard or what was bringing them joy. Through this process, I learned how impactful it was for students to be honest. Unlike other contexts where they might say they were "fine" and get on with it, something about our team and our ministry of presence meant that students could open up—they trusted us with whatever was going on in their lives at that time.

I continue to reflect on this practical wisdom. How do we create a space or a culture of care so that others may honestly share what is on their hearts—getting beneath the surface? This is the value of the meaningful check-in. Now, there is no formula. You can ask, "How are you? No, really, how are you?" and still get the same "Fine." It's not just about our words, however, it is about our posture. What is the energy that I am putting out into the world? How do I communicate with my body, eyes, and facial expression that I am with you? I am here and honestly curious about how you are doing. For instance, if I hold my phone in one hand, periodically look at push notifications, or checking the time, I am not demonstrating spaciousness or care with my time and capacity. Who would want to share something challenging or joyful if they have the conscious or unconscious suspicion that they may be interrupted? It's about vulnerability and trust. The protector within all of us is looking out for those moments. The protector in all of us wants to ensure that we do not make ourselves vulnerable in situations unworthy of our truth. Therefore, as aspiring listeners, it is our job to authentically communicate our availability and then create a container—in the physical space between us and our hearts—to hold what others share with deep care and respect.

LIFELONG WORK

My spouse has been a hospice chaplain for over fifteen years. He has his PhD in Practical Theology, has completed four units of Clinical Pastoral Education (hospital chaplaincy formation), and has taught and written book chapters on pastoral care. Knowing his professionalism and depth of experience, I am inspired and heartened by his commitment to honing his craft. A few years ago, while opening a package of new books from our field, he told me, "I am always working on my active listening skills. It isn't something that is ever done." His words reminded me of the concept of *shoshin*, or *beginner's mind* in Zen Buddhism. Beginner's mind is a foundational teaching in Zen that invites a whole reorientation of how we encounter the world—not with rigidity and hubris but with humility and compassion.

When we are new to something, we bring fresh, open eyes and ears. We are free of preconceived assumptions or weighty expectations—for ourselves and others. Instead, we engage with curiosity, bringing an exploratory sensibility. We are more mindful and pay attention to detail. We might be disoriented or feel like a fish out of water, but that is part of the learning experience. In the words of Shunryu

Suzuki, author of the landmark text *Zen Mind, Beginner's Mind*, "In the beginner's mind there are many possibilities; in the expert's mind there are few."[13] When I think of active listening skills, I think of the beginner's mind and the ongoing opportunity for learning that each day presents us.

In Christianity, Jesus calls us to similar thinking, living, and being. We see this teaching expressed most clearly in the Gospel of Matthew. As chapter 18 begins, the disciples approach their friend, hoping he will settle a debate among themselves. "Who, then," they ask Jesus, "is the greatest in the kingdom of heaven?"[14] In response to this status-obsessed question, Jesus calls them (and us) to a childlike faith, "Truly I tell you, unless you become like children, you will never enter the kingdom of heaven."[15] The commentaries often point out that in antiquity, children were not valued as they are today.[16] This contextual detail helps us better appreciate the point Jesus is making. He does not simply scold them for being too focused on power and status; instead, he directs their attention toward those who are overlooked—the exemplars in their midst, children. This passage becomes another example of Jesus's inside/out and upside/down vision of the world. Just as the first shall be last, the child shall be the teacher. A childlike faith is one steeped in humility and wonder. It is an existence free of the pretension and self-obsession we hear in the disciples' question. Because active listening is a lifelong skill, and can feel so at odds with how we are used to engaging with others, it takes time. We must be patient with ourselves. It is not our fault that these skills are hard to develop. They challenge the mainstream culture. Like prayer, active listening operates on a different rubric or set of values.

NANCY'S CONVERSION

I was sitting in the passenger seat of Sister Nancy's car when she told me the story. One of her students recently came out to her as transgender. I remember the moment clearly. She was still processing the experience and her pastoral response.

"It is so real," she said as she made a turn onto a Boston side street. "This student is sitting in my office describing what it is like to not feel at home in their body. I mean, can you imagine? Just try for a second. It sounds so hard. I have no idea what that is like. How could any of us who have not experienced that even begin to understand? I have so much to learn from this young person. They are terrified of losing their family; they are heartbroken to have lost their faith. They long for the Eucharist but won't attend Mass because they don't feel welcome. What they're going through—it sounds like hell."

This exchange is so memorable because it changed how I thought of chaplaincy and the lifelong work of learning from and being present to those around us. It revealed the side of this friend and mentor I had never seen before. Nancy was two years from retirement, having been a Roman Catholic sister since her early twenties, serving in many different ministry contexts. Here she was, in her late sixties, face-to-face with a whole new pastoral care situation. Her humility and compassion moved me deeply. She did not need to understand this person's pain; as someone who has not endured such suffering, how could she? But she did what she could—she listened, witnessed this student's truth, and honored their dignity.

As Nancy has told me, this story is one of conversion. Conversion is not always a 180-degree turn but a turn toward conscientization. Nancy turned toward conscientization as a result of her deep listening. In the ten years since Nancy's first conversation with that student, she has responded to the call. She asked her religious community and was granted a sabbatical to learn how to minister to transgender, nonbinary, intersex, and gender-expansive folks and their families. During those years, she traveled the country, getting to know community organizers and educators who are doing this important work. These days, she offers her workshop, "Transgender 101," for religious communities, parishes, and beyond.

"I was so ignorant," she says, reflecting on herself. "That conversation changed my life." Nancy continues this lifelong learning through conferences, workshops, support groups, and university courses. She is also very aware of her identity as a cis-woman and an older white nun and how her presence may affect others, especially those who have experienced harm at the hands of the Church. She is the oddball when she attends these sessions. And if the opportunity arises to reveal that she is a sister, folks move even farther away! But she is okay with that.

"It was about learning, and I had to shut up anyway, so I didn't mind," she told me. "I would just go to places where I was uncomfortable and listen. I got used to being uncomfortable, and now I'm not uncomfortable in those settings, but more importantly, people trust me."

CONVERSION IN DM

Dialogue and Mission, one of the postconciliar texts we explored in the last chapter, holds deep appreciation for conversion. It reads, "In biblical language and that of the Christian tradition, conversion is the humble and penitent return of the heart to God in the desire to submit one's life more generously to him. All persons are constantly called to this conversion. In the process, the decision may be made to leave one's previous spiritual or religious situation in order to direct oneself toward another. Thus, for example, from a particular love the heart can open itself to one that is more universal. Every authentic call from God always carries with it an overcoming of oneself. There is no new life without death as the very paschal mystery shows. Moreover, 'every conversion is the work of grace, in which a person ought to fully find himself again. (RH 12)" (DM 37).

I am particularly drawn to this image of leaving one's context—"previous spiritual or religious situation"—to "direct oneself toward another." It takes courage and trust to do this. One must be willing to be uncomfortable, enter the unknown, and trust in God. This is faithful work and work that will change us, expanding our hearts. I think of Nancy, who could have never imagined her retirement as it has unfolded. She followed God's call, leaving behind what had been and turned toward her student and to those on the margins who have endured harassment, threats of violence, dehumanization, and even bullying unto death. Surely, there is something wrong with how we operate if the status quo has led to such acts. Surely, we must do something differently if we hope to honor dignity and be in solidarity with all on the margins. Nancy never claimed to have all the answers, a formula, or a cure—she simply showed up for people, listened, and allowed herself to be changed by their beauty and truth. As is further explored in DM, "In the Christian view, the principal agent of conversion is not man, but the Holy Spirit" (DM 39). This insight should keep us grounded in humility, knowing that we are in God's hands, moving by the current of the Holy Spirit.

In a recent conversation, Nancy said something that really stayed with me: "I didn't learn about unconditional love in the convent. I learned about unconditional love from parents of trans kids." The Holy Spirit, as usual, works in unexpected places and in ways that often surprise us. Here is a question for each of us: are we awake to the Spirit in our midst and the ongoing invitations to conversion? This, too, is lifelong work. So, perhaps it is no wonder that a seasoned religious sister who has dedicated her life to living among the people and serving others would honor her conscience—responding to this immediate pastoral need—with such clarity, grace, and integrity.

Each day, we are greeted with opportunities to learn with and from those different from us. Whether it is a sibling who has had a different experience with our parents or someone from the other side of the world, the gift of conversion is the gift of invitation—to be challenged and changed, to have our hearts opened like Lydia and Nancy. We are called to honor the complexity of those around us and not to feel like we need to understand every detail but to hold sacred the truth that others share.

That day in the car with Nancy marked a conversion experience of my own. She modeled to me that we are forever being shaped and molded into the servants God wants us to be. That is, if we are awake to the call, willing to listen with our hearts and if we—like Mary and Lydia—say yes to the spirit. In the years since that conversation, I have been inspired by updates on Nancy's journey. Through the pandemic and orthopedic surgery, she has never stopped building connections with the transgender community and with trans folks who have no community. Her story reminds me that to be of service, we don't need to have all the answers; we just need to acknowledge what we don't know, listen to our brothers, sisters, and siblings, and be willing to be changed.

SPIRITUAL PROVOCATION: *LISTENING TO THE MUSIC OF OUR LIVES*

One winter evening, I invited our Interfaith Student Council to experiment with active listening through music. The prompt was to *think of a song or piece of music that you had spoken to recently or had spoken to you.* We then split the students into pairs and sent them to a quiet spot in the building. Thanks to the miracle of smartphones, they each took turns playing their musical selection. Nestled in the corners of our meeting room and peppered throughout the first floor of the building, pairs of students sat close to one another, listening intently, their eyes gazing softly at the carpet or out the window. Once the piece of music ended, the person who selected it started to reflect. They shared the origin story—how they first encountered the piece. They talked about who the song reminded them of, where, and under what circumstances they listened to it. They described the way their relationship to this piece has shifted over time. Through storytelling and story receiving, they brought their selection to life, giving it context and placing it in conversation with their truth. Then, they changed places, and the listener (the other partner) shared their piece of music.

When we ended the semester, the memory of this evening surfaced in several reflections, both implicitly and explicitly. Implicitly, we heard in their writing a deep appreciation for getting to know one another through these intimate storytelling experiences. Explicitly, we heard in not so many words that they were upset they could only choose one song! The beauty of learning active listening is that we get to employ this set of skills in all moments of our lives. When our friends are sharing a joy or a sorrow, when we are awash in live music or walking home before a thunderstorm, the leaves dancing with each gust of wind. We can use active listening when we are upset with someone in our family—a parent, sibling, or partner. Instead of rushing into the predictable patterned behavior, what happens if I try to withhold judgment and listen beneath the surface to what this person is saying?

While this chapter has included several exercises or spiritual practices—guided meditation, silence, storyteller/listener—I invite you to experiment with active listening in daily life. When you are at the supermarket and the clerk seems tired or overworked, when your colleague is venting, or when speaking with a neighbor about each other's gardens. Stay awake to how your internal landscape changes in these moments—how are you changed by listening more intently? Does your deep listening change your feelings toward this person? The point is not to make everyone in your life feel uncomfortable, like they are playing the role of your listening guinea pig, but to implement these practices into our lives to be more grounded, connected, and empathetic members of our communities.

CHAPTER FOUR

Sacramental Consciousness and Participation

In the previous chapter, we explored listening deeply to our inner landscape, one another, and God. This chapter focuses on listening to (and into) the lived sacramental tradition at the heart of Catholic spiritual life. It also addresses our call to participate in the living, breathing work of the Church. Whether implicitly or explicitly, I often hear students reflect on living a bifurcated life—they have a spiritual life and then the rest of their lives. It makes sense that we would think about these things as separate. Very often, these different realms are oriented around different sets of values and vastly different relationships to time and worth. In this chapter, our guiding question is how to place the richness of the Seven Sacraments in conversation with the everyday sacramental moments surrounding us. Living a wholehearted life as a Catholic means working towards a more integrated existence—one life. Like actively listening, however, this too is ongoing work.

One of my main goals in higher education chaplaincy is inviting students to embrace their whole life as a site worthy of reflection and reverence. As Catholics, I think this starts with expanding our sacramental consciousness so that we learn to see and appreciate the sacrament-full world in which we live. This richness is often untapped, and if we are to appreciate friendship—and interfaith friendship in particular—as a sacrament, then we need to unpack this terminology and the imaginative. Let me begin with a story.

THE HOLY IN THE EVERYDAY

We were so excited for my son to start kindergarten. He would be at this school for the next six years, and after the lockdown and a muted social life, I was thrilled by the prospect of all of us making new friends. We were among the first families to arrive on the first day of school. My son, R, insisted that we wait near the fence at the back of the blacktop. There he stood, taking in the scene before him—the old brick school building, smiling administrators with lanyard name tags, and the PTA's table of coffee and donuts. The schoolyard was full of little orange soccer cones, lined up in rows like desks—each one represented a different classroom. When he was ready, we found the cone for room 110. There was one family already waiting. Their little boy stood in his fresh haircut with his oversized Spider-Man backpack hanging off his shoulders. He was a walking patchwork of black, red, and blue—a Miles Morales color palette. I looked to R, a fellow lover of Spider-Man, and gestured to him to introduce himself. He was hesitant and nervous at first, as most children are on their first day, but once the conversation got going, they never stopped talking!

Something special grew that morning. They were two boys on the cusp of a new era of life, blessed with a shared love, something in common that they both held dear and could explore and delight in together. As they entered school that day, we could not have known just how pivotal that moment would be in our lives. In a few short months, this boy would change how my son understood "family"— it wasn't just about being biologically related; family was so much bigger than that. School was where their friendship took root, but it bloomed into many dimensions of our lives. At the playground after school, another layer of connection unfolded. Kindergarteners from both classes would pour out across the street with their parents. I marveled at the intimacy that took shape over those early months of the academic year. How quickly the children came to know each other! They knew the foods their classmates loved and loathed, which grown-ups picked them up, bus numbers, and if they went to the gym for after-school care. They were thoroughly steeped in each other's lives, awake to the details of the routine around them and the quirks that defined their personalities. A whole culture and community was forming each day, and we, the grown-ups, saw just bits and pieces when they surfaced in our presence.

One day, I got a peek into this beautiful, organic process. Standing on one side of the park, I could see that my son was getting upset with some of the big kids barreling through the pirate ship playground. He was about to storm off behind the concession stand when a girl in his class, a friend he often played with after school, saw me looking on.

"He does that when he's mad," she assured me. "It's okay."

She was right. It was okay. He took a break from the crowd and then returned more clearheaded. This moment was so revealing to me. This girl knew my son well; she could anticipate his frustration, how he would express it, and what it would look like. She was a keen observer and an emotionally intelligent five-year-old. I was so moved by how she took in the information and distributed it with nonjudgment. *That is my friend, R*, she seemed to say. At that moment, I realized the impact of this budding classroom culture. These children spent so much time with one another! For six and a half hours each day, they were in each other's midst—interacting, playing, negotiating, fighting, learning side-by-side. They were steeped in one another's presence, sharing space and building community one friendship at a time.

By the end of the year, my son and his best friend—the boy he met that first day—had become close. Their friendship expanded our lives, bringing our families together at the park after school, the movies (the new Miles Morales movie, obviously), and our kitchen table, where we shared meals after long spontaneous playdates. Those everyday moments were indeed sacramental, but they felt even more profound given the previous three years of pandemic restrictions and the ever-present fear so many of us had that we might spread or catch the virus. Andrew, a hospice chaplain, was visiting the homes of dying patients each day, which meant that we were extra cautious—the risk of spreading Covid-19 to a person already in a vulnerable position was too great. As we slowly emerged in the fall of 2022 and spring of 2023, receiving friends into our home was one of the greatest gifts. This boy and his family were some of our first guests.

Before vaccines, when churches were still closed, I wondered if the pandemic might be the impetus we Catholics needed to expand our sacramental consciousness. Perhaps this rupture would seed a more holistic experience of religious imagination and remind us that our faith can and must thrive outside of the liturgy. Would we heed the call to bring everyday sacraments into conversation with the Seven Sacraments of the Church? No longer able to receive the Eucharist at in-person liturgy, would we be in deeper solidarity with folks worldwide who only receive the Eucharist once a year—a common experience for those living in more remote regions? Would we take a closer look at our dinner table and remember that it, too, is a site for eucharistic meals?

I had high hopes for what was to come and the impact of the pandemic restrictions on our religious imaginations. While I am not expecting a revolution (though maybe I should), I am hopeful that we may still come to our senses and begin to engage meaningfully with the wisdom we gleaned from this time. I recognize, however, that this is hard. The desire to return to business as usual seems to have eclipsed any momentum for innovation. Many longed for the "before times "or were anxious to settle into the "new normal." Being away from community took a toll. We missed grieving together and celebrating joys together. We missed taking up space in one another's physical company. I understand that desire to 'return' even as I experience nostalgia for the different perspective that time afforded me.

In the fall of 2022, I had a conversation with a young woman who spoke longingly of her parish's virtual house church, which met during the lockdown. She described what it was like to share reflections on the gospel with other layfolk—many of whom were women. They brought such insights and exciting reads to the text. Each week, they took turns facilitating different parts of the service. She and her mom even baked communion bread. It is not every day that a high schooler enthusiastically shares stories of innovative liturgy! But there I was, listening to a wise woman reflect deeply on a period that changed her understanding of what it means to *be church*, be the body of Christ. She spoke of a genuine sense of *alleluia*, giving glory to God in community with one another. That phone call was such a gift.

When the conversation shifted back to reinhabiting the sanctuary in post-pandemic liturgies, the disappointment in her voice was not so subtle. She missed those experiences of deep connection and learning. She missed the co-creative spirit and seeing everyone in their homes—a strange intimacy that somehow brought us closer in our apartness. She was communing with her fellow congregants in ways she could not have imagined. This young woman was used to being one of the token young people in her congregation, but those intergenerational gatherings enriched her spirit, offering a window into the depth and wisdom of the layfolk around her. And she wanted more of it.

The summer before returning to graduate school, I took a class at Boston College School of Theology and Ministry. The professor was Richard Gaillardetz. I had no idea how lucky I was to get a chance to study with him. Rick, as he asked us to call him, was an esteemed professor of systematic theology, a Vatican II scholar, and a former president of the Catholic Theological Society of America. I had wandered into that class as a training session, getting myself ready to write papers again after a ten-year hiatus from graduate school. Little did I know how formative that course would be for my thinking around spiritual formation. When he found out I had an infant, Rick invited me to bring the baby whenever I wanted or needed. Naturally, the next week, my spouse had a pastoral emergency, so R and I sat on the side of the classroom, sharing a blanket of toys and snacks for the duration of the class. In this context, I was introduced to a critical way of thinking about religious education, spiritual formation, and what Gaillardetz called "the fetishization of the Sacraments." This language was new to me, but I knew what he meant. I have seen this transactional dynamic play out in many settings. Years later, in speaking with that young woman, I would hear in her voice the hunger for something more—something beyond the consumeristic model that has sadly permeated our church culture.

In religious education, we have directed almost all our attention toward the Seven Sacraments. We have also employed pedagogical methods that have followed the classroom culture of the American school system far more than the Holy Spirit.[1] This narrow experience of our sacramental tradition is perpetuated and strengthened by the absence of substantive formation around mystagogy, the lifelong work of sinking deeper into the mystery of the sacraments and adult catechesis.[2] The students I meet are often hungry for multiple entry points into their spiritual lives. Amid the freneticism of life with supercomputers in their pockets and color-coded calendars playing Tetris with time, students report feeling relieved, comforted, and excited by the invitation to see God in the everyday moments. They don't have to wait for that rectangular hour on Sunday to pop up to feel connected to their faith; they can live into this sensibility all week. God's ongoing invitation to be in relationship with us is something to celebrate! In the words of Jesuit theologian John F. Baldovin, "God doesn't communicate his life to us despite our created, physical, human condition but precisely in the midst of it."[3] God is as close as each breath we take throughout the day.

Defining Sacrament

Before we go any further, we must pause on this term: *sacrament*. Augustine's words from the fifth century have been the standard definition: "an outward visible sign of an inward invisible grace." These words might roll off the tongue for some, but how do we keep ourselves from being numb to the profundity of this language? I recommend embracing Richard Rohr's insight as regards the Trinity—that we are "endlessly understanding" this mystery. We may find ourselves more agile and supple if we can bring that spirit of humility, lifelong learning, and unlearning into this conversation about sacraments.[4]

In her beautiful book *Becoming the Sign: Sacramental Living in a Post-Conciliar Church*, Kathleen Hughes calls our attention to the expansive sacrament experience. It is not just the single moment in the sanctuary when the baptism takes place; it is part of a longer, contextual story. She writes:

> The sacramental rite is simply the public, ecclesial acknowledgment and celebration of what has *already* been going on in the life of the individual or group; the ritual deepens the experience and enables the individual or group to live the experience more fully and faithfully into the future *following* the public celebration. There is a ritual celebration of a sacrament that happens in the midst of the process of sacramental living; the sacramental rite is radically continuous with the sacramentality of the day-to-day. To think otherwise is to make the sacrament a kind of magic moment.[5]

In this passage, Hughes paints a powerful picture of interdependence—sacramental rites (the events) unfolding within the greater context of everyday sacramentality. Her phrase *the process of sacramental living* invites us to reflect again on the movement or dance that captures the energy of the Holy Trinity. I hear a dynamism and a sense of patience in Hughes's words. It is, after all, a process. In our desire to consume and digest tradition, we can get frustrated that we have not figured it out yet. I see this in my chaplaincy, where students expect to take on overly ambitious Lenten practices with perfection! They are used to excelling and expect themselves to quickly grasp complex concepts and theology and employ them in life. Some hold themselves to a near-impossible standard with a rigidity that can impede spiritual growth. But spiritual life is not like a syllabus. It is gnarly, nonlinear work. It is all about process and experience as ever unfolding.

Expanding Our Sacramental Consciousness

When I was an undergraduate, the library was the place where I went deep. I would work my Sunday night shift at the Circulation Desk from 9 p.m. to midnight and then wander into silent study for another few hours of quiet. The religion stacks were on the lower level, in the far corner, a womb-like undercroft with no windows, but rich with nourishment. For a religion nerd like me, it felt holy, imbued with an ineffable sense of possibility. I bring those memories with me to every library I visit.

One afternoon a few years ago, I was writing at a Catholic college library, and when I needed a break, I started to roam the stacks. Writing can be so lonely, and I was hungry for that embodied experience of connection and wonder. There, I came across a little life-changing book by Leonardo Boff. I had been reading his work on the Holy Trinity in seminary, but this publication looked different—a sore thumb at my eye level. This skinny blue paperback from the 1980s casually shared a shelf with hardbound theological books—a glimmer of brightness interrupting the march of brown and maroon tomes with their reflective gold titles. When I took the book off the shelf, it was out of curiosity. "What are *you* doing here?" I asked. The cover was a pencil-drawn kitchen table still life—a torn loaf of bread, a red metal cup, and a cigarette butt. Indeed, what *are* you doing here? I had no borrowing privileges at this library, so I spent the rest of the day devouring this wee book in a study carrel beside a window overlooking the quad.

The Sacraments of Life and a Life of Sacraments was a transformative read for me. Boff put into language what I had been feeling for years. Our lives are full of these moments of sacramental rupture, but are we awake to them? His deep reflections on seemingly ordinary objects reminded me of the Jesuit call to find God in all things. As I made my way through the chapters, each story demystified the cover art further. The drawn cigarette butt represented the last smoke to touch his father's lips. In an expression of sacramental love and care, Boff's sister enclosed it in the letter that broke the news of their father's passing. Her brother, who was studying in Munich, received the gift with deep gratitude. Years later, Boff would explain that "from that point on, the cigarette butt ceased to be a cigarette butt. It became a sacrament and remained one. It is alive and speaks of life. It accompanies life. Its typical color, its strong smell, and its burnt end mean it is still lit in my life."[6] The cigarette butt, the coffee mug, and his mama's bread communicated a deep sense of connectedness and meaning—all events revealing God's grace. Boff modeled how these ordinary objects could be doorways to the sacred with a slight shift of perspective.

I experienced Boff's writing as a spiritual gift—a Holy Spirit moment. Not only had he given voice to a way of being in the world to which I felt called, but he also affirmed my place and sense of ownership in the tradition. As a laywoman, I felt seen, welcomed, and celebrated. I felt his warm embrace through the words on the page. He wrote:

> The sacraments are not the private property of the sacred hierarchy. They are basic constituents of human life. Faith sees grace present in the most elementary acts of life. So it ritualizes them and elevates them to the sacramental level.... God was always there, even before we may have been awake to the fact. Now that we are awake, we can see that the world is a sacrament of God. People who manage to perceive and appreciate the sacraments of life are very close to, or rather already immersed in, the life of sacraments.[7]

What is most compelling and comforting to me here is the reminder that God is always with us, accessible in our skin, bones, and inner life. Sacraments are right here in front of us, gifts from our God of Abundance, our God of Surprises.

This spiritual posture takes me back to high school geometry class. Sitting in those rows of desks, a sheet of paper in front of me, trusting—knowing for sure—that everything I needed to solve the problem was on the page. The teacher had given us just enough information. I simply had to figure out *how* to think about it and use what was already there to tell a more complete story. Creativity, perception, agency—it is all within our reach. But how do we exercise those muscles of observation and connection?

One of the great joys for me in chaplaincy is introducing students to diverse practices for meaning-making. We connect to God, self, and others through movement, contemplative prayer, walking meditation, praying with art, the psalms, and everyday elements of our lives. These are just a few of the tools in our toolbox. I learn so much from students when they share about their prayer life—how they learned to pray with their grandma or feel connected, across time and space, to family during our multilingual rosary circles. Catholic theologian Andrew Greeley calls this "the Catholic imaginative," capturing the deeply sacramental consciousness that comes through imaginative engagement with aesthetics and story.[8] The mysticism in Boff's writing points toward the breadth and depth of this central part of our tradition. Students come alive when we unpack this posture. They are eager to be invited into this rich component of the tradition and to grow in spiritual maturity. Greeley's work on the Catholic imaginative acknowledges the richly poetic inner world of laity. He employs the term *enchanted imagination*, arguing that the laity have historically remained the curators of the tradition's texture. This read is even more noteworthy given the fact that the culture of clericalism has privileged rules and hierarchical power over imagination, art, and story.

Feminist theologian Mary Hunt suggests a profound dynamism in the sacramental imagination. She explains that

> to sacramentalize is to pay attention. It is what a community does when it names and claims ordinary human experiences as holy, connecting them with history and propelling them into the future. . . . It is simply taking time to attend to the people around us, to see in real lives (not in novels nor in Scripture) the stuff of human existence: birth, pain, growth, bonding, breakup, loss, friendship, and to recognize it as such. This is what sacraments are for. They are concrete experiences

with food and touch, dance and drink, prayer and silence, affirmation and music. Think of a good dinner party. What could be holier? How one-dimensional much of what passes for sacraments in church is by comparison. [9]

Hunt dispels the binary thinking that has led to so much dangerous theology and empty practice. She blurs these lines by bringing embodiment and lived reality into focus, which has historically inspired isolation and self-doubt. When our daily lives are not seen as the holy sites they are, they are shoved off into the land of the profane; the land of *this doesn't count*, or *this is not holy enough*. To sacramentalize is to reject the cultures that have kept us apart from one another and from seeing, feeling, tasting, and delighting in the sacred surrounding us.

When I teach about sacramental imagination, I often turn to Andre Dubus's beautiful essay "Sacraments." Dubus, a twentieth-century American writer, describes the state related to this kind of living, Boff's kind of living, as a "receptive condition."[10] He models this hospitable heart and imagination by mapping out the sacramental act of making lunch for his daughters. Dubus, who was paralyzed in a car accident in 1986, brings his reader into the details of his life—the micro-movements in his kitchen routine, the order of operations necessary to account for the range of motion in his wheelchair. He writes, "A sacrament is physical and within it is God's love; as a sandwich is physical and nutritious and pleasurable, and within it is love if someone makes it for you and gives it to you with love; even harried or tired or impatient love, but with love's direction and concern, love's again and again unwavering and distorted focus on goodness, then God's love too is in the sandwich."[11] He goes on to narrate the choreography of his sandwich making—each muscle movement needed to open the drawer, obtain a plastic bag, the curl of the knife spreading the mayonnaise. These motions are all part of a grander dance, a Trinitarian dance. Dubus's expression of love to his children is something they will consume—embodying the Eucharist in action and intention.

Hunt, Dubus, and Boff emphasize that we can only truly encounter and appreciate these sacraments if we have cultivated an inner landscape that is oriented toward the holy, if we are in touch with our bodies and the sensuousness of existence. This receptive condition is a posture. It prepares us to pay attention, fostering a spirit of hospitality and generosity. From that place of rootedness comes the capacity for spiritual innovation and imagination.

Dwelling in the Enchantment

The first summer of the pandemic, I took my then three-year-old to spend the day at the beach. We were up early, as usual, and the two of us hit the road. If you have ever gone to the beach with a small child, you may know it is not a particularly relaxing experience. There is no reading with the waves rolling behind in the distance. No dozing off in the warming sun, belly on the sand, face nested in a towel, shaded by a floppy hat. It is super fun, do not get me wrong, but it is also, more or less, a nonstop loop of sunscreen application, snack distribution, sandcastle construction/destruction, water safety everything, and, of course, sand toy envy.

By the time it was early afternoon, I was exhausted from playing all day, but we had to go back to the water one more time before leaving. The ocean was calling our name. I carried him out past the breakers, and we floated together, bobbing up and down in our sun hats, laughing as we narrated the sea moment by moment: "Oh, here comes another big one," I'd say, his entire body wrapped around me like a monkey. It was a moment of profound connectedness—expanding beyond time and space.

I felt deeply connected to my mother, who taught me how to swim in the ocean, diving under those Jersey shore waves. I felt connected to my body and the sacred act of laughing with someone you love. When I looked out at the horizon of Narragansett Bay, I sensed for an instant the immensity of God's grace, so moved by the beauty of creation and the miracle of our own capacity to delight in this beauty.

One thing was clear: This was a baptismal moment. We were renewing, cleansing, and clarifying. Of course, there was still so much to come with the pandemic, but those first few months of lockdown were hard. The loneliness, isolation, fear, disease, the loss of embodied worship, the loss of human life, the further revealing of fault lines, systemic racism, and other deep inequities in our society came to the surface. Being away from others during that time of acuity made it all the heavier to hold and bear. In the water, however, I thought about my last communal worship experience. It had been Ash Wednesday in Goddard Chapel that first week of March. We were beginning our time in the wilderness, a wilderness most of us had yet to imagine. It felt like a world away. But that day on the beach, we were in a holy assembly, surrounded by strangers, clouds of witnesses, breathing together—safe beach breeze breaths, resting in the joy of creation.

That experience continues to reveal to me the gift and challenge of placing the Sacraments of the Church in conversation with the everyday sacramental moments in our lives. This is how we live more wholeheartedly as Catholics. It is not my spiritual life and my regular life . . . no, it is one life. A single existence where these experiences—in and outside liturgy—mutually inform one another, shaping how we understand our identity as people of faith.

Once I started embracing this way of being in the world—this orientation—I realized I was living in a sea of sacramentality. For instance, a few years ago, a young alumna returned to campus to speak with students about her vocation as a community advocate. However, the most powerful part of our evening together was her impromptu reflection on her and her friend's weekly ritual as students at Tufts. In the fall of their sophomore year, these two women began meeting for coffee after class each Thursday. It started organically as a co-caffeination project of convenience, but they quickly found their friendship deepening. Those long conversations nourished them for the week, and they committed to showing up for one another every Thursday for the next three years.

Sitting over coffee with a stranger-turned-friend was a sacramental encounter for these young women. It was transformative—the holy breaking through as they paid close attention to the person and world before them, working hard to truly *see* one another. These two women were open to the spirit of spontaneity. They were open to the process of learning to listen. Eight years after their initial meeting, they shared that table once again on the eve of their five-year reunion. They booked their flights into Boston with the summer hours of the café in mind, which was, in essence, an expression of reverence—their time together was sacred, that place was sacred. They did not allow fear of being known to keep them from this profoundly formative and meaningful connection. They opened themselves up to vulnerability and to truly being seen.

Watching this alumna tell the story of her friendship was yet another extension of the sacrament. Current students eagerly listened to her frame as holy something that seemed so ordinary—getting coffee with a friend. The sanctuary of the campus café was a place they each knew well, but had they ever thought of it as a sacred space? This moment of testimony stretched the imaginations of the students present. For those who had never thought this way, she offered a pathway into another way of being. Sometimes, an imagination problem needs a spark of disruption to wake us up to the spirit and help us cultivate our receptive condition.

One Sunday a few years ago, I witnessed one such receptive condition grow before my eyes. Due to a scheduling mix-up, we learned last minute that we would not have a priest for our 5 p.m. Sunday Mass. At 4:58 p.m., I spoke with the choir and we shifted the hymns for a Liturgy of the Word. While it was disappointing and stressful in the short term, such evenings were rich, teachable, and transformative moments—a reminder that we are just a bunch of human beings gathering to give glory to God. On this particular night, a young woman named Rebecca was in the congregation. I could see that she was deflated and confused by the priest's absence. At the end of the liturgy, however, she approached me beaming with energy and excitement. This young woman gushed about how powerful it was to gather around word and song to pray with one another. She added, "Of course, I came for the Eucharist, but this was awesome. Different but awesome."

In those words, I hear so much. She is like so many of us—hungry for the Eucharist but living with a narrow understanding of what is eucharistic. She was always so present to the celebration of the Paschal Mystery but she had never experienced a liturgy of the word. She and her friends used to sit in a row, shoulder to shoulder, in the choir loft, bobbing their heads, holding hands, and dancing as we sang the Lord's Prayer. These visible signs of their joy within the Mass were infectious. However, that night's experience opened her up to different ways of encountering the holy through sacrament and community. Not just the Liturgy of Eucharist toward the end of the Mass, but the act of being together, witnessing to one another, and trusting the spirit to guide us.

These three women, Rebecca and the café crew, teach us that there is more to being an observant Catholic than simply attending Mass as a consumer—taking in the Sacraments in a transactional way. There are opportunities throughout our day for deep and meaningful connection, and they are holy. The disruption of that Sunday evening and those long hours at the coffee shop are reminders that together, we are the body of Christ—not just when we stand in the communion line. We move toward a more holistic and integrative life as a disciple by placing these rich threads in conversation, allowing them to inform and shape one another mutually.

OWNERSHIP AND MISSIONARY DISCIPLESHIP

When I began reading the Vatican II documents *Lumen Gentium*, *Apostolicam Actuositatem*, and *Sacrosanctum Concilium*, I was in awe. As a layperson and a woman in the Church, I felt seen and appreciated—I felt worthy of taking up space. It was nothing short of transformative. Here were the texts that affirmed the active participation of laity in the sacramental life of the Church. But I was also confused. Why had it taken so long to be face-to-face with these beautifully written documents affirming the gifts of all the baptized? I was a religion nerd who had gone to divinity school, a

Catholic who had gone to Mass every Sunday with my family, and I had never encountered this part of the tradition—either in text or practice. Of course, I experienced the ripple effects of Vatican II, as most North American Catholics in the late twentieth and early twenty-first centuries, but the vision has never been fully realized.

When Pope Francis released his 2013 apostolic exhortation *Evangeli Gaudium*, it felt like a new breath of life. The spirit of these earlier documents was present and taking a new form. One passage in particular has been a compass for me in my work. Pope Francis writes, "In virtue of their baptism, all the members of the People of God have become missionary disciples (Matt 28:19). All the baptized, whatever their position in the Church or their level of instruction in the faith, are agents of evangelization, and it would be insufficient to envisage a plan of evangelization to be carried out by professionals while the rest of the faithful would simply be passive recipients."[12] In settings like mine, where there is so much emphasis on achievement and excellence, it is helpful to remember that the work of the missionary disciple is not concerned with such material world measurements. As Pope Francis says, it does not matter what level of instruction one has regarding the faith, but how our encounters with Christ guide each of us.

One of my favorite things to remind students is that while they are honing academic gifts and interests to be used out in the world for justice and mercy, parts of each of us fall way outside these lines of "excellence," and God is using those well. It is not about romanticizing our sufferings and trusting that they are all part of God's plan, whatever that means. It is about affirming that we are complex human beings and that the Spirit is moving through us in our messiness. In the paraphrased words of Lutheran pastor and writer Nadia Bolz-Weber, God uses all of you, not just the stuff you're good at.[13]

Our student leaders consistently report that their newfound place in ministry at Goddard Chapel is a genuine surprise. When alums reflect on their roles in the Catholic Community at Tufts, they often say they would have never imagined being so integral to the Catholic landscape. They had no experience of ownership in their home parishes. Some could not imagine a rich spiritual life, let alone inspire others as a spiritual leader. This is a particular symptom of the culture of clericalism, and we see here how it bleeds into the personal faith lives of laity, keeping their worlds small, limiting their imaginations for what is possible, and having a chilling effect on their call as missionary disciples. Some students reflect on feeling at once undervalued and overextended, cast into the role of the stereotypical young person who holds the key to making the Church more relevant. I saw this dynamic unfold in real time on an interfaith trip several years ago. What follows is a story of clericalism and a case study of one of my missteps as an interfaith leader.

It was Sunday morning in August, and I was accompanying a religiously diverse group of students on a sanctuary field trip to a Catholic parish in Boston. We were in the midst of a week-long program aimed at building relationships and religious literacy. These students had already been to a Sikh Gurdwara, a Hindu temple, and a synagogue. This site visit was supposed to be easy—just a T ride away to a congregation I had attended off and on for years. After the service and tour of the building, we debriefed in the basement with the well-meaning pastor, an acquaintance of mine. Before we got too far, however, I sensed it would be challenging. He made several side comments about the number of students who did not identify with a particular religious or philosophical tradition—his voice bore a tone of judgment. Then he made a flippant remark about Humanism and I took that opportunity to tell him—and the many first-year students present—about our robust Humanist Chaplaincy. I explained how students who are nonreligious or atheist or living without labels have found a meaningful home in that community.

I thought we were heading into the meat of the conversation I had envisioned, but then it took another turn. The pastor asked all the Catholics in the room to raise their hands. One student from a Catholic-Buddhist interfaith family did so, and he asked the question, "How do we get more young folks to come to Mass?" This student leader, so thoughtful and courageous, shared her frustration. "I felt tokenized at my home parish," she explained. "I was in the choir and on parish council, and I was asked that question endlessly." I was in awe of her. She spoke so candidly and authentically. However, instead of listening to this student and acknowledging how this dynamic had affected her, the pastor accused her of avoiding the question. He then interrupted her and asked again: "How do we get more young folks to attend church?"

In just a single moment, this experience revealed to me the multidimensional and transactional nature of clericalism—the priest's actions and my reactions. Internally, I was fuming. His question and confrontational nature were appalling. I selected this site because it seemed like the kind of community that would understand the goals of interfaith work. I thought I had communicated our hopes for this conversation, but maybe I hadn't. I could feel my internalized clericalism rising within me and was grateful for the student's courage and witness. I envied her resolve. I felt capable, composed, and convicted when addressing the interfaith lens, educating about Humanism. However, when the conversation shifted to the Catholic lens, I folded in on myself. I was the chaplain for this community, but I allowed this priest to steer the conversation in hurtful and, frankly, inappropriate ways. Was I afraid of him? Why else would I let him dominate like that?

Eventually, I redirected and recovered but was ashamed that the experience had taken that unexpected turn. I wish I had said, "Thank you for proving her point," but I was stunned into silence and was relieved to move on. When we returned to campus, we had a substantive processing session to address the situation, but at that moment, I felt like I had let our students down. Looking back now, I have more compassion for myself, and the irony of it all feels more instructive than a sign of personal failing. I have learned so much over the years reflecting on that half hour gathering. It is a reminder that in this work, we make mistakes, but they are sites to mine for practical wisdom. In my professional development as a chaplain, this incident helped me understand the push and pull I experience internally depending on which hat I wear—interfaith leader and/or Catholic lay minister. It also affirmed my deep love and respect for the work of my Humanist colleagues in chaplaincy. I was proud to be an ambassador and educator, and I am so grateful to learn with and from them every day.

The clericalism displayed by the pastor continues to disappoint me. At the very moment when one would expect hospitality, a religious leader trying to say, "We care about you," he took it as a chance to extract an answer, a formula, a magic spell, a cheat code. And yet, we are all human. I know that he has seen the landscape of his congregation change dramatically over the years. He is not alone in wanting answers. Like many, he is worried, anxious, and maybe even feeling a little desperate. I empathize with those afraid of these massive cultural shifts, but the pastor's question was and continues to be the wrong one. My friend Regina, an Episcopal priest, has put it beautifully: *"How do we get people, and especially young people, to come back to church* is an idolatrous question. The questions we in the Church should be obsessed with are: *How do we become the Church God longs for us to be? What would it take to get there? What would we have to give up and let go of, and what would we have to take on and commit to get there?"*

The first time I heard my friend ask these questions, we were sitting across from one another at a well-worn wooden café table. The bookshelves around us climbed toward the industrial ceiling, and I felt myself sink deeper into my chair—how I had longed for this reframing. She had just articulated something I had tried to understand for years. It was a great comfort to turn away from the metrics of the material world and to be awake to the dreamings within us and the voice of the Spirit. It is countercultural, prophetic, and, for some, too radical, but I see it as the most faithful and realistic reframing of communal call. The deep humility in this posture continues to inspire me. None of us can know where these dreamings will lead us, but as God's people, we must trust that the Shepherd will lead us to the next green pasture and the next tiny tuft of grass that will nourish and sustain us.

Jamie's Story

Jamie's story is one that I hope will serve as a guidepost in this conversation about ownership and the need to empower the laity. Jamie was one of our stellar student leaders from her sophomore year onward. Across campus, she was involved in peer health movements, social justice activism, Catholic life, interfaith engagement, and athletics. When she graduated and stayed at Tufts to work on her master's, she was intentional about her presence in the chapel community. Given her previous leadership in the undergraduate student group, she wanted to ensure she didn't overshadow any budding leaders or create a dynamic wherein the younger students deferred to her. I appreciated her careful discernment and how she honored our community's culture, but I always made sure she knew she had a home at the chapel. That summer, between finishing one degree and starting another, Jamie began exploring the parishes in Boston. She approached this challenge as she approached all things—with curiosity, eagerness, and an open heart. One afternoon, walking to Davis Square, I ran into Jamie. I was excited to hear about her experiment in other congregational settings and to learn if she had landed anywhere. She told me about one parish where she had started attending Sunday Mass regularly. She had even tried out for the choir and was thrilled to share that she made the cut! Then her voice turned inquisitive.

"I am trying to get involved in interfaith work in Boston, so I visited the Greater Boston Interfaith Organization website. But when I scrolled down, I didn't see my parish listed," she said. "In fact, I only saw one Catholic Church on their list of member institutions. Does that sound right to you? Am I missing something?" She let out a long exhale, and her shoulders sank. "Where are all the Catholics?"

Jamie's genuine confusion spoke volumes to me. Her experience of interfaith engagement had grown from the context of her spiritual life *within* the Catholic community at Tufts and the wider University Chaplaincy. These worlds were both separate and deeply connected. As her chaplain, I had the wonderful privilege of watching her place her Catholicism and interfaith posture in conversation with one another. I followed her in awe as her passion for community health, spiritual development, and religious literacy were meaningfully shaping one another. Before the pandemic, she was asking questions about how to frame public health campaigns to speak to different cultural contexts. What role do religious sensibilities play in how individuals, families, and communities think about vaccines or sex education? When Jamie began discussing these issues, her whole being changed. She was always the caring, passionate, and genuinely curious woman I loved, but you could see that this work ignited something else within her. It was transformative. It was a calling. She was called to do this work—to bring her gifts, questions, and drive to this critical field. Perhaps that is why the confusion and disappointment in her voice that day was so memorable. I can still hear that deflation and disappointment—*Where are all the Catholics?*

"That's a good question—a very good question," I said, letting the silence hang in the air. We kept walking, and eventually, I asked what was keeping her from gauging the interest in her new parish and suggesting they get involved in the Greater Boston Interfaith Organization. She paused and looked at me with an expression of surprise and bemusement. "I just got there. I'm new. Can I do that?" And then her voice dropped an octave and she answered her own question: "I *could* do that."

When this young woman was on campus, she was a pillar for the organizing efforts to support peer mental health. She challenged herself to grow intentionally, working hard to postpone judgment, to grow in compassion, and to listen deeply to classmates with whom she disagreed. She taught herself to "stay in the room" and not allow the conversation to devolve into a polarized debate or name-calling. It was genuinely challenging for her, as it is for all of us, but she wrestled honestly with this practice. As a person of faith and someone heading into a field rooted in relationship building, she was adamant about developing these skills. Jamie's experience in community organizing, active listening, and cultural humility meant she was well-equipped to help foster a burgeoning ministry in her new parish. I was confident that she would proceed with care and patience. She would first listen to the community and learn from them. She would not steamroll them with self-righteousness or shaming.

But I continue to be vexed by why it had never occurred to her that she could be the one to do it. I do not blame her. It is not her fault. I am grateful for her honesty and for her friendship over the years. She helped me see how clericalism stymies sacramental consciousness and innovation—even in the privileged, even in the most outspoken, empowered, and confident of people, clericalism infects and diminishes us. If even a strong leader, thinker, and organizer like Jamie can be unaware of her agency within the Church, then we have much learning and unlearning to do. We need the Jamies of the world to guide and inspire us. In speaking with her and other young folks looking to settle into parish life post-commencement, there is a sense that they will go elsewhere with their energy and passions if the Church is not ready to welcome them in.

Clericalism

I have many priests in my life who have been incredible mentors, friends, and colleagues. This section is not an attack on them but a way to address the sickness within our Church that has helped perpetuate unimaginable harm and inequity—through sexual violence, corruption, and other behaviors and attitudes that diminish members of the community. Layfolk, religious and clergy alike, can perpetuate clericalism. At its worst, it has led to insidious violations of trust through the abuse crisis and systemic cover-up. But it can also take forms so far from that extreme that we may be tempted to dismiss them.

I urge us to stay awake and call out those patterns and ways of thinking. They do not simply evaporate into the ether; instead, they are absorbed into our bodies and minds through micro-movements that impact our expectations of self and others—exemplified by my freezing in that scenario in the church basement. The passivity of layfolk in the face of clergy may seem innocuous. We know, however, that it diminishes the baptismal call of that lay person, withholding their gifts to the greater Church and contributing to the culture that places priests above—which was at the root of the abuse and cover-up. Our Church is steeped in clericalism, but that does not mean we must surrender to this dysfunction. Part of disavowing the fetishization of the Seven Sacraments of the Church and opening ourselves up to everyday sacramental moments includes unlearning the clericalism we have internalized.

For some readers, the term *clericalism* might evoke an image of a man in a Roman collar receiving special treatment or anecdotes of entitled or self-absorbed priests. While noteworthy in their own right, these examples do not capture the breadth and depth of this sickness within our Church. Clericalism is not about individuals behaving badly or inappropriately; it is about a system that creates the conditions that justify and normalize extreme power imbalance and dehumanization. To the bishops assembled for the Synod on Young People, Pope Frances explained that "clericalism arises from an elitist and exclusivist vision of vocation, that interprets the ministry received as a *power* to be exercised rather than as a free and generous *service* to be given. This leads us to believe that we belong to a group that has all the answers and no longer needs to listen or learn anything, or that pretends to listen. *Clericalism is a perversion and is the root of many evils in the church*: we must humbly ask for forgiveness for this and above all create the conditions to that it is not repeated."[14]

This term *perversion* hits me so hard. It comes from the Latin word *pervertere*, which translates as overturn or corrupt. It literally means *turn around* or *turn the wrong way*. This aberration or corruption naturally makes me think of the *right way* or what was originally intended. Many Vatican II texts mapped out the renewed vision for participation in the vineyard. The *Decree of the Apostolate of the Laity* was solely devoted to this topic. It frames the role of layfolk and the relationship between layfolk and clergy as such:

> As sharers in the role of Christ as priest, prophet, and king, the laity have their work cut out for them in the life and activity of the Church. Their activity is so necessary within the Church

communities that without it the apostolate of the pastors is often unable to achieve its full effectiveness. In the manner of the men and women who helped Paul in spreading the Gospel (cf. Acts 18:18, 26; Rom. 16:3) the laity with the right apostolic attitude supply what is lacking to their brethren and refresh the spirit of pastors and of the rest of the faithful (cf. 1 Cor. 16:17–18).[15]

Have you ever considered your work and presence in the Church as "necessary"? Have you considered your presence and ministry to be sharing in "the role of Christ as priest, prophet, and king"? These are powerful statements and ones that will take time to unpack. But let them be our guideposts in this work as we navigate our way through challenging terrain. As Francis has conveyed, solidarity and synodality are the antidotes to clericalism. Being intentionally together, listening to one another, understanding our liberation and humanity's liberation as intertwined with one another—that is how we will move forward into right relationship. This is how we will be open to the Holy Spirit moving in and between us.

In a 1977 homily, Archbishop Óscar Romero shared his dream for all the baptized:

> How beautiful will be the day when all the baptized understand that their work, their job, is a priestly work, that just as I celebrate Mass at the altar, so each carpenter celebrates Mass at the workbench, and each metalworker, each professional, each doctor with the scalpel, each market woman at her stand, are performing a priestly office! How many cab drivers I know listen to this message there in their cabs; you are a priest at the wheel, my friend, if you work with honesty, consecrating your taxi or yours to God, bearing a message of peace and love to the passengers who ride in your cab.[16]

The work of layfolk is not lesser. It is work out in the world. Take a moment and think about *your* work—whether in your family, community, or place of employment. How is this "priestly work"? In other words, how do you express your priestly service to others? Turning toward the language in the *Decree of the Apostolate of the Laity*, can you employ this lens to appreciate and lift up what you already are doing as holy work—priestly, prophetic, and kingly? By that, I mean, how are you reflecting faithfulness, spreading the good news out in the world, and caring for the Body of Christ? How might Archbishop Romero's passages inspire you to lean further into your call?

ANTI-CLERICALISM AND EQUIPPING THE SAINTS: UNLEARNING THE CLERICALISM WITHIN

In higher education chaplaincy, I think a lot about my students' needs in the present moment, but also how they will manage life and who they will be in ten, fifteen, or twenty years. In Paul's letter to the Ephesians, he writes from prison to frame unity as a virtue and remind the community of its greater mission. The gifts of God are to be used for the people of God. In chapter 4, Paul writes that Christ "gave the apostles, the prophets, the evangelists, the shepherds and teachers, to equip the saints for the work of ministry, for building up the body of Christ" (Ephesians 4:11–12). I think of this passage often. For religious professionals, what are we doing to "equip the saints" around us, and what does this equipping look like? In light of the need for cross-worldview connection, religious literacy, and empathy building, how might we equip layfolk to step into leadership roles to support interfaith work?

When I speak to friends and colleagues in the parish setting, they are often thrilled by the prospect of laypeople's energy and creativity. While each context is different, capacity is the most significant factor. My friend Lara told me there's a difference between "I've got this great idea, and I want to do it; I just need these three things" and "I've got this great idea, and I want YOU to do it." I laughed when she told me this because we see this too in chaplaincy. So much of our ministry model revolves around supporting student leadership. There have been times, however, when students have dreamed great dreams but have not made plans to execute the vision. In those moments, I must stop myself from swooping in to save the day. For example, if the cars were never reserved to go apple picking . . . then I guess we are not going. This is a rare dynamic; our students are usually very responsible, but every once in a while, we have to let a beautiful opportunity pass to serve as a teachable moment.

In the parish setting, where staff is stretched thin, and there are many pressing pastoral priorities, I can understand that interfaith engagement is low on the priority list. This all makes sense, especially in the wake of the pandemic, when so much energy was streamlined to tend to the acute needs of the moment. As we head further away from this time and are confronted with deep, divisive conflict and violence on American soil, Palestine/Israel, and Ukraine, now is the time to build a connection on the local level, expand our hearts, and ask that vital question: Who *is* my neighbor?

A recent study out of Santa Clara University explores the structural reality of clericalism. In "Beyond 'Bad Apples': Understanding Clergy Perpetrated Sexual Abuse as a Structural Problem and Cultivating Strategies for Change," Julie Hanlon Rubio and Paul Schutz define clericalism as a "structure of power that isolates clergy and sets priests above and apart, granting them excessive authority, rights, and responsibilities while diminishing the agency of lay people and religious."[17] They explain that systemic clericalism functions as "a system of incentives, restrictions, and enablements that is 'baked in' to every aspect of ecclesial life, of our community."[18] This vital qualitative research is based on interviews with the Catholics in leadership within parish settings—religious, clergy, and layfolk.

Toward the end of their study, Rubio and Schutz reflect on anticlericalism and, specifically, strategies for opposing this structural harm. Rubio and Schutz draw upon the work of Ibram X. Kendi and his framing of racism and anti-racism. Kendi's insistence that "racist policies drive racist thinking" offers us a way to think about the Church and how clericalist power imbalances infect all of our thinking, feelings, and actions on an institutional level. Rubio and Schutz found that in their interviews of ecclesial ministers, there were noteworthy examples of anti-clericalism. In terms of power, they note that "in contrast to theologies that place the priest above and apart from the rest of the Church and so grounded authoritarian management styles, anti-clericalist theologies emphasize openness to many voices and a recognition that ministry begins with authentic listening."[19] When we reject the status quo assumptions about where power resides within our parish communities, we live more fully into our baptismal call. As one respondent said, this allows for more innovation, creativity, and "being open to mystery."[20]

Every congregation is different. The management style of one pastor might lend itself to a collaborative spirit, while the same suggestion at a different parish might be met with great resistance. Fear of change and the threat of a multiplicity of voices might be too much for some in leadership. This possibility, however, should not deter us from following the call when it arises. In the Rubio and Schutz study, one priest respondent explained that "even among clergy of good will, men have been 'in charge' for so long, the clergy leadership is incapable of seeing what an inclusive church would look like. The structures are inherently sexist."[21] I found myself quite moved by this reflection as it reminded me of the way that those who benefit from systemic injustice—whether white folks in the case of racism or clergy in the case of clericalism—are also diminished and afflicted by these structures. The inability to imagine something new and thus being closed off to the Holy Spirit is its own form of loss and suffering. This way of being might be grievously impacting those around this person, but they, too, are also hurting—locked in an abusive system.

It takes courage to voice one's dreamings, but I have found that when one person comes forward with an idea on their hearts, they are often not the only one. You might be surprised in any number of ways—encountering apathy, opposition, or something in between. Remain faithful to the call within. In the wise words of a seminary classmate, God has already put it on your heart. In situations where I have found myself frustrated by resistance, I have made a concerted effort to inwardly return to the leadership style that Jesus taught us—servant leadership. Finding strength and purpose in serving others has helped rebuild my sense of purpose and connectivity. There are many entry points into interfaith work; stretching our sacramental imagination is just the beginning. We need to stretch the imaginations of our communities—this might mean just beginning a conversation, like Jamie in her new parish.

It also may mean living into a spirit of anti-clericalism and not waiting for an overworked clergyperson to care about it or have the capacity to take it on. You might begin by hosting a general interest meeting at school, establishing a more formal association or connection with a local interfaith organization, or taking on a more intentional internal posture toward difference. I recommend that we all begin by bringing that genuine curiosity, wonder, and deep listening to our interactions in our daily lives. Invite a colleague or neighbor out for coffee or a walk. These moments of communion are holy. They matter and are sites worthy of deep theological reflection and meaning-making.

SPIRITUAL PRACTICE

The ancient practice of Lectio Divina originated with Desert Mothers and Fathers as a way to be open to the living word. When we pray with scripture this way, we affirm that the text is always new, speaking to the present moment in fresh, spirit-filled ways. Lectio Divina has four components—reading, meditation, prayer, and contemplation. Less steps than process, they are akin to a spiral, layers of engagement in constant conversation with one another, circling as you grow closer to the center.

This practice is most effective with a relatively short passage. I have selected one below that speaks to the themes of this chapter, but perhaps you have one in mind that you would wish to explore and experience in this way. I invite you to experiment with Lectio Divina in private prayer spaces or with a friend or small group.

Suggested Passage (1 Corinthians 12:27–31)

Now you are the body of Christ, and each one of you is a part of it. And God has placed in the church first of all apostles, second prophets, third teachers, then miracles, then gifts of healing, of helping, of guidance, and of different kinds of tongues. Are all apostles? Are all prophets? Are all teachers? Do all work miracles? Do all have gifts of healing? Do all speak in tongues? Do all interpret? Now eagerly desire the greater gifts.

Begin by finding a quiet place and focusing on God's ever presence. Ask God to help you leave behind any expectations or agendas. Ask God to help open your heart and bless you with the grace to listen.

Reading: Slowly read the passage aloud. Remember that you are in no rush; you are just where you need to be—sitting with scripture in the presence of the Most Holy. Be open to any word, phrase, or image that is speaking to you today. Allow it to call your name. Sit with this word, image, or phrase and see where it takes you. You may choose to journal or sit in silence.

Meditation: Slowly read the passage for a second time. Let the words wash over you. Listen and ponder what has surfaced for you in the passage. Repeat your word/phrase/image and invite it to be in conversation with the particularities of your life.

Praying: Slowly read the passage a third time. Reflect back to God the conversation that is unfolding within you. As you repeat this pattern of speaking and listening, you may arrive at some clarity—what is

God saying to you through this word? If clarity feels elusive, that is okay too. Trust that the Spirit is guiding you and will continue to guide you.

Contemplation: Dwell in God's presence and receive God's warm embrace. Trust in the fact that language is a mere approximation when it comes to our relationships with the holy. Remember that being with God and carving out space for God is enough. Rest here, in this place, where God is acting in you.

CHAPTER FIVE

Humility, Courage, and Allyship

May was a first-year student from an interfaith family. While she primarily identified with the Catholic community, her Jewish identity was critical to her. During the spring semester, as we moved through Lent and every passing day brought us closer to Passover, she found herself full of longing—longing for home, tradition, and the connectedness she was used to experiencing during this holy time of year. May stayed awake to this stirring within her, and after some reflection, she decided to share her family's Passover Seder tradition with the Catholic community. Her pals on the Catholic leadership team were excited by the idea—no one had ever been to a Seder. To prepare, May reached out to one of the rabbis on campus, and over tea several afternoons, they came to envision the Seder together. The rabbi gave May a few options for the Haggadah, the book used at the Seder table to tell the story of the Israelites' escape from Egypt. She listened to what was on May's heart and guided her in this journey of shared spiritual practice.

I remember the joy in May's voice when she told me about the impending trip to the grocery store to buy food for the Seder plate. She could not wait to chop apples for the charoset, even if it meant squeezing into the tiny galley kitchen she shared with every resident in her dormitory and using suboptimal cutlery![1] When Holy Thursday came around, May seamlessly stepped into a place of religious leadership. She taught her Catholic friends to sing Dayenu, walked them through the ritual foods on the Seder plate, and reflected on what the experience of the Passover Seder meant for her and her family. Later, she shared that it was one of the few times in the year that her father would don his tallit (prayer shawl). In those moments, she felt connected to her ancestors, who fled the pogroms in Eastern Europe, and her grandmother, who continued cooking peasant food in the United States—warm bowls of comfort that May held dear.

May would host a Seder for the Catholic community for the rest of her time at Tufts. Constantly feeling that pull between her Catholic and Jewish identities—questioning her worthiness in each setting—May was brought to a place of integration through these evenings and the sacramental preparations. She was seen as the whole person that she was. She would adapt and adjust each year, incorporating practical wisdom from the previous year and bringing more friends to help. She brought pastoral agility and humility to the process. These are spiritual gifts that I continue to reflect upon many years later and that I see in full bloom as she has answered the call to congregational ministry, serving as ordained clergy in the United Church of Christ (UCC).

It is right to be suspicious of Seders in Christian contexts. Churches have long appropriated this central Jewish tradition, further compounding the deeply problematic and violent threads of antisemitism embedded within the fabric of Holy Week. UCC pastor and theologian Rev. Dr. Mary Luti reminds us, "It is no accident that many a medieval pogrom erupted during Holy Week. It was a time rife with anti-Jewish preaching that placed the blame of Jesus' death on Jews—not just on the ancient Jews, but on all Jews—and, in some cases, directly called for unsparing violence against them."[2] Facing this challenging, deeply painful, and harrowing history, especially during Holy Week, is critical work for Christians. Luti and many others have called out the practice of so-called Christian Seders for years now, providing a nuanced explanation for the many hurtful dimensions of this religious and cultural appropriation. Holy Thursday Seders send a particularly damaging message that the

Seder's value is rooted in Jesus's redefining it as a eucharistic meal. The greater backdrop of the "Christian Seder" is an assumption that Judaism was the incomplete, unrefined precursor to Christianity.

I was unwittingly introduced to this supersessionist mentality early in my formation through the lens of theologies that painted Jesus as the liberator of women. Embedded within this narrative is the unchecked and inaccurate portrait of Judaism's oppression of women. Within ministry contexts, I have also heard youth ministers refer to the God of the Old Testament (Hebrew Bible) as a vengeful God, contrasted by that of the New Testament, who is framed as a God of love and compassion. I mention these examples here to reveal the many layers of anti-Jewish thinking that are baked into how Christians tell their story. We may not be fully conscious of the ways that antisemitism has shaped our tradition. Still, we are responsible for bringing that awareness and history into our lived experience of faithfulness. In the words of Luti, "Our anti-Jewish history has 'earned' us a particular responsibility to make sure that our embrace of the Jewish heritage is serious, respectful, self-conscious and well-considered. We may not borrow, play-act, adapt, or otherwise appropriate anything Jewish like a Seder without carrying with us unto that activity this whole history."[3]

I lift up this vital criticism side-by-side with May's offering to the Catholic community. More generally, these situations—and multifaith observances—deserve our attention and careful analysis. As I will demonstrate, they are sites of ongoing learning, and if we are steeped in the spirit of humility, we can participate in this learning as we go, adjusting and pivoting when needed. This kind of agility and resistance to fragility is necessary for cultivating meaningful interfaith relationships. While absolutely in a Christian setting, May's Seder was a gift offered to friends from her hybridity. It was not an example of "play-acting"; instead, she invited her classmates into her reality, into the aspects of her life, and into multivalent identities that were meaningful and profoundly affirming. Because it came from her and this place of deep reverence and authenticity—and created in partnership with the rabbi, a professional religious leader—it was not voyeuristic or exploitative but a transformative gift of experiential learning and religious literacy.

In her book *Stealing My Religion*, Dr. Liz Bucar offers a way to think about religious borrowing and how to name and engage with Christian hegemony and other power structures that can lead to religious minorities feeling undermined, offended, or even attacked. She does not employ the term "religious appropriation" to cast moral judgment—which often shuts down conversation—but as a way to explore the ethical dimensions of borrowing from other traditions. She argues that religious appropriation is far more complicated than cultural appropriation, given the porous lines of religious identity. Bucar, whose critical self-reflections include acknowledging her stealing of religion, invites her readers to unpack the many dimensions of these examples and weigh the potential harm against the benefits. She writes:

> The hardest thing about religious appropriation is that the solution to the forms of ethical harm it creates is not simple avoidance. Avoiding religious borrowing is impossible, given the way religion is consumed in the American context. It might also be undesirable because it could prevent forms of meaningful engagement. What we need instead is a way to understand when religious borrowing entails hidden exploitations that are grounded in broader forms of structural injustice, and what we might do to mitigate these harms.[4]

While one could make the case that May was not borrowing because she was from a Jewish/Catholic family, it is true that her primary religious experiences and spiritual formation took place within Catholic contexts. But to say she was only Catholic would have missed the mark, and indeed, she said herself that when she was viewed this way, she felt incomplete, unseen, and like she wasn't honoring her patrilineal family. Honoring May's identity reminds us that none of this is black and white. Instead, these details and dynamics demand more critical reflection from us.

This brings me back to Bucar's point about meaningful engagement and the gains of such border crossings. In this instance, the Seder proved a transformative experience, one that built a bridge for Catholic students who were allowed to learn experientially about Passover in a way that did not invade or co-opt a Jewish space during this holy time of year—something that could have unfolded had they all had simply attended the Seder at Hillel. May modeled a genuine spirit of humility. Knowing what she did not know, she turned to the rabbi who walked with her and helped her craft an offering that would be substantive and truthful to her values and questions. I know that this mentorship/friendship with the rabbi was a significant part of May's spiritual life at Tufts and to think that her loving gift to the Catholic community came from this collaborative partnership makes it all the more meaningful.

This story also shows how May was open to growing and evolving her thinking. With each passing year, she made critical adjustments to the Seder, the meal, how to tell the story, and who to include in the telling. Ten years later, when I spoke with May, she said she would do it differently. She acknowledges that her sense of urgency in that moment—to be seen and whole—no longer resides within her. Naturally, this would be the experience of a nineteen-year-old in the weeds of identity formation. As a woman in her thirties, she now holds different values, needs, and perspectives. Through self-critique and ongoing learning, she has arrived at a new place and has consciously decided not to organize Seders as a pastor in her congregational setting. Given her role as a Christian religious professional, it would be inappropriate for her to do so, but I do not see that as reflecting poorly on her Seders on campus. That was a different time and place. These days, she operates from the comfort of her hard-won wholeness, rooted in her Christian tradition, even as she delights in attending her spouse's synagogue. May's careful approach and reflection model a drive for ongoing crafting and reshaping. This should inspire us not to be foiled by fragility and fear of making mistakes but to move into the community with grace and intentionality, open to ongoing conversion, revision, and reimagining. We are changing human beings in complex contexts—internal and external. One size fits all does not do justice to the kind of nuance and deep listening required for this work.

For the Catholic community, the Seder ended once May graduated. The tradition's home resided within her, and she had moved on. However, this culture of lifting up the wisdom and diversity within the community remained. A few years later, a student from Hong Kong would lean into this spirit of generosity, inviting classmates to his apartment for a Lenten simple supper. Like May, he prepared for days, and on that Friday night, he cooked his mother's absolutely gorgeous (and decidedly not-so-simple!) recipes from back home. Abundant plates of whole fish, bean curd, and vegetables filled the table that evening, and the students present gushed about that meal for weeks. His expression of hospitality was reciprocated by the warm reception of his classmates—hospitable hearts in all directions.

When preparing for interfaith work, we must operate from this place of deep care and contextuality. Each relationship, indeed each moment, is of a particular set of complexities and deserving of intention. We must consider our positionality and identity when engaging in interfaith work. Historically, Christians have dominated spaces. Given the greater context of colonialism and Christian supremacy, we have a responsibility to be conscientious of our power and privilege as we inhabit and hopefully help create religiously diverse spaces. How do layfolk take initiative and step into leadership while also being mindful of not taking up too much space? *This* is the work. I have no answers or formula, but I can say that it is a series of constant conversations—within ourselves and in community with others. At the heart of it all, this work requires humility.

This chapter turns toward the practical application and addresses how Catholics can approach interfaith work morally and ethically. How do we reach across divides, honor the dignity of religious others, not perpetuate harm, and grow into genuine allyship? How do we be thoughtful participants, sharing from the rich particularity of our tradition without taking up too much space—as Christians and, specifically, as white Christians have done in the past? I hope that these questions will prompt us to be intentional and thoughtful. They are not intended to have a chilling effect on individuals or organizations, scaring off anyone eager to explore interfaith work. Instead, they are an invitation to inhabit the place of introspection, contextuality, genuine curiosity, and humility that we see so beautifully conveyed in May's story.

FROM THE TRADITION: THE GIFT OF HUMILITY

The word *humility* comes from the Latin word *humilis*, "from the earth," "of the ground," or "grounded." The same root gives us the words *human* and *humor*. We are of the earth or dirt, so humility means being down-to-earth or earthy.[5] Many of us may struggle with this word. Experiences of abuse and oppression can cause this word to feel re-traumatizing, pushing you down yet again. Bad theology has no doubt functioned to keep people of color and women from places of power, pushing them away—to the margins, into submission, and justifying it as some kind of God-willed system. It is important to honor this reality and acknowledge the profound challenge of this word. These feelings are real and valid.

However, when I speak about humility, I draw from a liberative tradition. Humility is not humiliation. It is not about overly pious observance or reinforcing structures that dehumanize. Instead, it is a way of being in the world that acknowledges our humanness, our deep need for relationship, and the reality that we do not know all. Humility is about being open to transformation, as with beginner's mind, humility allows us to bring fresh eyes to our lives and relationships. In their research on humility and social justice, Dawn Moon and Theresa Tobin write, "Humility is not simply a character trait, but a disposition rooted in concern to protect relationships, giving deeper meaning to our understanding of human beings as social creatures."[6] This disposition is something that can be honed and cultivated. Tending to relationships and honoring the dignity of those around us invites us into a more profound sense of belonging.

Moreover, free of constricting assumptions, we can live in a spirit of genuine curiosity. Staying awake to the movement of the Holy Spirit requires this posture. The spontaneity of the Spirit can surprise us, leading us to new places and prompting us to engage with playfulness.

Humility and gratitude are deeply related—they remind us that we are connected to something greater than ourselves. When I am grateful, I am awake to the web of existence that has brought me here. When I give thanks for a meal, for instance, I acknowledge my connection to and reliance upon the farmer who grew the produce, the irrigation team, the person who drove them to work, and whoever made their breakfast. I am aware of my inherent connection to the person who stocked the shelves at the grocery store and our next-door neighbor who shared her grandmother's recipe with me. These folks and countless others helped bring the meal to my table. I cannot do it alone, and to forget this litany of cocreators dishonors their contributions, gifts, and sacrifices. In many ways, humility is like that as well. I cannot know it all, but I must be open to learning what I do not know. My existence is inherently interdependent with others, and I am called to acknowledge how they help shape my understanding of the world and how I engage with it.

Father Jon Uni of Saint Cecilia parish in Boston Back Bay often reminds his congregation that "we all came from the good God, and we're going back to the good God." I turn to this short statement quite often. Personally and professionally, I find deep comfort in these words. They remind me that I dwell in the bosom of God. I am known. I am loved. Others are known. Others are loved. So much is outside of our control, but we are part of God's creation, formed in clay by God's hands. As Richard Rohr notes,

> The word "human" comes from the Latin humus, which means earth. Being human means acknowledging that we're made from the earth and will return to the earth. For a few years we dance around on the stage of life and have the chance to reflect a little bit of God's glory. We are earth that has come

to consciousness. If we discover this power in ourselves and know that we are God's creatures, that we come from God and return to God, that's enough. As a human, I'm just a tiny moment of consciousness, a small part of creation, a particle that reflects only a fragment of God's glory. And yet that's enough.[7]

The final words of this passage from Rohr are bound to challenge many of us: "And yet that's enough." This countercultural orientation contradicts our capitalist sensibilities that tell us more is always better. It is not unlike the beatitudes—that inside-out, upside-down vision of the kingdom of heaven. Where the first shall be last. What is it like to reside in this enoughness? How does the reality of our brief existence shape our everyday interactions with others? Do we feel connected to the stardust or anxious about our legacy . . . or lack thereof?

KENOSIS, OR SELF-EMPTYING

As we dwell with humility and consider the role of Christian privilege in this society, the theological concept of kenosis serves as our guide. *Kenosis*, or *self-emptying*, refers to Jesus's way of being in the world. In Paul's letter to the Philippians, he paints a picture of Jesus's self-emptying:

> Let each of you look not to your interests, but to the interests of others. Let the same mind be in you that was in Christ Jesus, who, though he was in the form of God, did not regard equality with God as something to be exploited, but emptied himself, taking the form of a slave, being born in human likeness. (Philippians 2:4–7)

This passage was inspired by one of the early hymns of the Church.[8] In some circles, it is even referred to as the "Kenotic Hymn."[9] Just imagine early Jesus followers lifting up some version of these words in song. Many voices becoming one to proclaim a prophetic expression of communal identity, mutual relation, and reciprocity—this deep value of looking toward Jesus's sacrifice invites us to sit with our call to sacrifice, to be in true solidarity with one another.

In chapter 2, we spent time with a passage from *Nostra Aetate*, which alludes to these famous verses from Paul. "The mind of Christ" calls us into a place of generosity and self-emptying. Counter to our individualistic culture, kenosis invites a Trinitarian consciousness, seeing our deep interdependence with one another and how we might relinquish power to be in right relationship—allyship. In her book *The Church Cracked Open*, Episcopal priest Reverend Stephanie Spellers explicitly connects Christ's self-emptying and our call to relinquish power—to empty ourselves—to serve justice. She writes that "as individual Christians, faith communities, and institutions, we can practice kenosis and release our hold on false narratives, privileges, and self-centric structures built to serve empire, White supremacy, and the established order. Let die what needs to die, so that God's new creation can be born."[10] Relinquishing control takes courage and humility. It takes trusting others to step in and lead and letting go of our grip on power. It requires learning how to be an intentional and thoughtful follower of religious and racial minorities.

Christian supremacy and white Christian supremacy are so baked into American culture that it can be challenging for some folks to see it. While this is not okay, it is understandable. If you are someone who cannot see it yet, I implore you to bring patience, vigilance, and an open heart to this work. For starters, this is how power and privilege operate. For those in the dominant culture (Christians and white folks), it is the water in which we swim that makes it hard for us to see it. If we are to embrace an ethic of cross-worldview friendship, however, we as Catholics need to recognize our complicity in systems of oppression and commit to emptying ourselves of the need to take up space—or to get in the first word or last or to be comfortable at all times.

Kenosis is the essential nature of Jesus. To be in relationship with others—religious others, cultural others, social pariahs—he had to relinquish status quo conceptions of kingly power. In the words of Episcopal priest and womanist theologian Kelly Brown Douglas, "Jesus divested himself of anything that would obstruct his complete solidarity with the most oppressed and least of these in his society. Essentially, he denounced his claims to patriarchal, ethnic, or even religious privilege."[11] When we honor kenosis as foundational to Jesus's identity, he becomes our roadmap to imagining solidarity and allyship in our churches, schools, and communities. Returning to chapter 3 and our conversation about active listening, we find deep resonances with the spirit of humility, guiding reciprocity, and kenosis. Catholic priest and theologian Henri Nouwen wrote, "Someone who is filled with ideas, concepts, opinions, and convictions cannot be a good host. There is no inner space to listen, no openness to discover the gift of the other."[12] How might we become good hosts to others' stories, laments, hopes, and hurts? How will we work on emptying ourselves of cultural scripts that oversimplify, silence, or dehumanize?

These questions get at the heart of the Catholic Social Teaching Principle of Solidarity. This foundational social teaching of the tradition is based on the truth that we are all part of one human family. Each of us is responsible for tending to one another, honoring and promoting the dignity of our brothers, sisters, and siblings. In the words of Pope Francis, "Solidarity means much more than engaging in sporadic acts of generosity. It means thinking and acting in terms of community. It means that the lives of all are prior to the appropriation of goods by a few. It also means combatting the structural causes of poverty, inequality, the lack of work, land and housing, the denial of social and labor rights. It means confronting the destructive effects of the empire of money."[13] We must also consider our internal conversation with Pope Francis's words in mind. How have our perceptions been warped? As human beings living in an unjust world, are there obstacles impeding our capacity to see and respect others as our human family? What would it look like to divest from this thinking so we may show up and be in solidarity with neighbors from other traditions or no tradition? These are the questions I ask with my anamcara, Heather.

THE ROLE OF THE ANAMCARA

When the lockdown began, my soul friend Heather and I laughed at how our relationship felt strangely unchanged. We had lived about an hour away from each other for several years, so we were used to only speaking on the phone. Almost once a day, though sometimes more, we check in, witnessing to one another's life—celebrating joys, lamenting in solidarity, raging at injustice, meandering through the mundane, and sharing moments of beauty and wonder. I take good notes throughout the day, so when I speak to Heather next, we can laugh at something absurd or savor an experience of awe.

She is a fellow religious professional, which is a great gift. I can turn to her when I need perspective and honesty. When I fall short in chaplaincy or life and need to understand better how I missed the mark, I call her and pour over the details of the incident. As a white woman, I must be intentional about unlearning the racism within. As a laywoman in the Church, I need to do similar work in terms of clericalism. Heather has been a comrade on this path. She is someone with whom I can speak openly as I reckon with these sinful parts of myself. This soul friend has a way of pushing me to grow while also offering a deep embrace. We are a home for each other, which allows us to be raw and honest, reckoning with the parts of us that diminish others and ourselves. It is necessary to wrestle with these questions with honesty and vulnerability. How else will we be able to move forward and in solidarity if we do not have a reliable and unpretentious container for the unlearning?

CHRISTIAN PRIVILEGE AND WHITE CHRISTIAN NATIONALISM

Many Catholics might think that the culture and history of anti-Catholicism provides an exemption from Christian privilege, but this is not the case. Anti-Catholicism indeed continues to be a meaningful presence in the United States, but it is not nearly as fierce as in past eras, when often collapsed into an anti-immigrant mentality. With Catholics in the White House and in the majority of the Supreme Court, those days of hiding behind anti-Catholicism are behind us. Catholics—and white Catholics specifically—benefit from the structures in America that privilege Christian customs, calendars, and countless cultural touchpoints. If Catholics are to engage ethically and morally in interfaith work, we need to be actively decentering Christianity. This means bringing a deep awareness to the structures at play—to the way that our culture has privileged Christian identity—and reorienting ourselves in such a way as to disrupt these patterns. It is possible to do this work while also being true to our faith.

I see this as leaning into the truth of the Trinity. Difference is holy. Difference brings us closer to oneness. It is not enough to create a program, gathering, or offering and simply invite folks from other traditions to attend. This approach is an example of centering a Christian worldview, and it is a far cry from partnership. In coming together and building friendships across tradition, the goal is to be challenged and changed, to see the holy from an entirely different point of view. That will require relinquishing power and stepping back from leadership to follow the vision of religious minorities.

The following short story is a single example of Christians missing the mark. While a seemingly small oversight, it shows how we can unconsciously privilege our perspective and culture, which, at best, can make some folks feel less welcome and, at worst, be downright alienating and violent.

In divinity school, I attended an interfaith gathering at a local church. While the vast majority of guests were white Christians, there were several Muslim and Jewish folks present as well. The evening began with hors d'oeuvres and drinks, but many of the options laid out on the counter of the church basement included various beers and wines. I imagine this decision was made with the best of intentions. Whoever was in charge of the drinks wanted to offer a range of beverages and was probably used to always offering alcohol. In an interfaith setting, however, alcohol is a massive barrier, as many Muslims abstain from drinking alcohol as well as being in the presence of it.

Had this event been planned in community with all the neighbors, a conversation regarding dietary needs and appropriate offerings would have most likely occurred in the spirit of a genuine partnership. There may have been another person in the room who might have also raised the issue of serving alcohol in a mixed setting where there might be folks in recovery from substance use. The point is not that the beverage purchaser is a bad person but that the event's whole orientation failed to embody the spirit of co-creativity it sought to create in bringing folks together. If raised and explored, these concerns could have served to educate, deepen empathy, and help foster a more authentic communal identity.

In his essay "Not in the Name of Jesus: On Being True to Ourselves," Hussein Rashid encourages us to think deeply about the role of power and honest discourse in interfaith work. This rich case study follows two experiences he had with students as a Muslim scholar in residence at an Episcopal seminary. I could not possibly do justice to the nuances and richness of these stories—I highly recommend reading his essay and the entire collection *With the Best of Intentions*—but his final words serve as instruction and invitation. He writes, "In addition to the often-unacknowledged questions of power, there are also limits to politeness. Attempts to be overly cautious for fear of offense without consultation with our partners, keep us in the same place. We do not get to know one another, discover one another, and engage with difference."[14] I appreciate how Rashid prioritizes authenticity and ongoing communication. He wants those in community with him to be honest about who they are.

In the one instance that Rashid cites, students had muted parts of themselves and their observance for his sake—omitting Jesus language in a prayer session. When he found this out, Rashid felt diminished because he had "not been consulted and was unaware of the limits they had placed on themselves. They still had control of the situation, and were having me expose myself, while they concealed part of who they were."[15] These students were trying to be conscientious, but in so doing, they had perpetuated the old song of a Christocentric framework, making the decision themselves.

When Rashid reflected on his debrief with the students, their moment of clarity and consensus centered around the question of what helps build "open and transparent relationships."[16] This short phrase serves as a guidepost and a reality check. How do we create the conditions for openness and transparency? Beyond who is in the room, where is the door, and who knows its location? It can be easy to fall back on our familiar constructions of what is a religion. This is a big question and one that I cannot address here. Still, I mention it to bring awareness to the vital roles that SBNR (Spiritual But Not Religious), earth-based spiritualities, healing traditions, and Indigenous practitioners play in this work as well.

THE ROLE OF COURAGE

In a 2023 interview reflecting on white Christian supremacy, Fordham professor Father Bryan Massingale celebrated the courage of ordinary Americans resisting demeaning and dehumanizing structures in their day-to-day lives and context. He told the story of the Black women poll workers in Georgia who refused to let the harassment they endured deter them from keeping the polls open and the junior white house staffer who spoke truth to power at the January 6th hearing. Fr. Massingale invites us into the spiritual dimension of this work. "Courage is a virtue," he reminds us. "We as Catholics say that it is a gift of the Holy Spirit. And I think we need to do better not only teaching people to be politically discerning but forming people in the virtue of courage and willingness to do the right thing despite being afraid."[17]

When I hear these words from Father Massingale, I think of the powerful relationship between courage and humility. To speak out in the face of hate requires that we are willing to acknowledge that we, in God, are beyond the structures of this material world. After all, when we act with courage, there is a risk of loss—loss of power, money, prestige, or relationships. But ultimately, these things are fleeting, paling in comparison to the great gains—integrity, authenticity, and faithfulness. It is our conscience and our faith that are of the things that last.

Deacon and theologian William Ditewig writes that "courage is active. . . . Moral courage, for example, describes a person who takes the right action despite any and all opposition. Courage is not passive, simply enduring something; courage acts to change, defend, and move forward into the unknown."[18] This emphasis on movement takes me back to our conversation about the Holy Trinity and the dance in and between the three Persons. This Trinitarian dynamism echoes the dance I see between humility and courage. We must be grounded, rooted in a vision and a mission "in order to do the right thing despite being afraid," as Father Massingale would say. And, of course, it takes courage to live prophetically—"to do what is right, to love mercy and to live humbly with your God" (Micah 6:8).

By naming and facing religious bias and discrimination, we are disrupting the culture of white Christian nationalism—we are taking "the right action," and we are embracing courageous humility. After all, any dishonoring of human dignity requires a swift and firm response. When we act in this way, we are creating an alternative narrative. We are moving toward solidarity and rejecting the inherent assumption that we are okay with hate done in our Christian name. In racial justice work, sometimes this is referred to as *cheap solidarity*—a white person assuming another white person holds the same prejudices and biases as they do. This triangulation is a cheap way of building connection, as it seeks to normalize hate and to bully others into normalizing racism. If the other person does not share those views, the dynamics of the situation are such that it is on them to "make the moment uncomfortable," pushing back on the racist rhetoric. Moments like this require the kind of courage of which Father Massingale speaks. Whether this is in the context of anti-Blackness, antisemitism, or anti-Muslim hate, we are called to speak up and help foster healthy spaces that honor human dignity.

INTRA-FAITH FRIENDSHIPS

Even amid the discomfort or awkwardness of interfaith encounters, these experiences afford a special kind of comfort or safety. The differences across traditions are so significant that the threat to one's perspective can often feel remote. Disputes and disagreements are more pronounced and explosive *within* our traditions. As a result, interfaith work can even feel like a reprieve from these internal tensions! Professor Harvey Cox explains in his book *The Future of Faith*, "As conditions worsen, we feel ever more uncomfortable talking with co-religionists who—many of us believe—distort and demean what we both share. Sibling rivalry is the nastiest kind. In the first murder Cain killed Abel over the proper way to sacrifice to the God they both worshiped. The rivalry between the brothers was an intrafaith dispute."[19] I find a strange comfort in Cox's reminder that one of our earliest stories lifts up this particular kind of challenge. After all, it is because the brothers both care so deeply that the offense is so great. That said, we have the opportunity to learn from their story and to tell a different one. We can both empathize and imagine a new story.

The American Catholic Church often feels as polarized as the political landscape in the United States. I am not usually on Catholic social media, but when I occasionally check in, I am gutted by the comments. Siblings in Christ take each other down, attacking one another's expression of faith, seemingly intending to belittle and demean. Usually, such vitriol is based on the assumption that there is only one way to be observant. In this global Church, where Vatican II has called us to celebrate our unique contexts as revealing the beauty of God's diverse creation, I am pained by our seeming incapacity to hold complexity or multiplicity with deep care. Fault lines tear at the seams of families who once attended Mass together but can no longer venture into dialogue because it feels too dangerous. Like Cain and Abel, we care so much.

Perhaps you have someone in your life or parish with whom you disagree. Maybe it is a difference in how you worship, practice your faith, or prioritize Church teachings. Sometimes, we can fall back on the assumption or mantra that this person is impossible to talk to. I understand that hurt is real, and you might have drawn a boundary for your own safety or mental health. It is important to honor that. As I affirm whatever measures you have taken, let me dream for a moment. In contexts where safety and mental health are not in question, what would it look like to employ the skills of active listening and story-sharing with our Catholic and Christian siblings with different ideological, theological, or ecclesiological perspectives? What if it were not about dialogue but about listening and taking on a posture of genuine curiosity and wonder? What if it was heart work, not head work? It would take courage, vulnerability, and trust, but what if we took out any subtext or pretense of trying to convince the other and focused only on building connection and empathy? In the words of Sikh activist Valarie Kaur, what if we thought of everyone we met as not a stranger but "a part of me I do not yet know"?[20]

It is important to note that not everyone will be a fruitful or healthy conversation partner. When folks have demonstrated that they are in neither the head nor heart space to engage with generosity, I support stepping back and directing your precious energy elsewhere. No one deserves to be criticized, attacked, or demeaned. Continuing with this theme of capacity and context, I recommend also thinking deeply about the communities that nourish and sustain you. It is okay to refill your cup within the contexts that provide you spiritual fulfillment before returning to building relationships across differences. I would lift that practice up as a critical part of self-care and community care. I have no answers or formula, but I know that I have learned so much from Catholics with whom I disagree immensely. When there are no personal attacks and instead a lens of curiosity and reverence, we have inspired one another on the journey of faith. If this feels too hard right now, I invite you to lift it up to God in prayer. Try talking to God as you would a friend, naming the fears and the hurts. This is lifelong work; we all need the Holy Spirit to guide us.

SHOWING UP AND STICKING AROUND

There are moments of acuity in our world and our communities when the most important thing for us to do is to show up. In the immediacy, this might look like attending a rally to support a religious community that has been under attack or whose safety has been threatened. It could be joining forces to support a collaborative effort for housing or healthcare access—issues that affect folks in vulnerable situations across identities.

Showing up in the moment is imperative but so is sticking around. When I say "stick around," I don't mean overstaying our welcome, becoming a burden, or violating the sacred space of an affinity group. I mean taking in the long view. What does allyship look like for the long haul? If you have ever lost a loved one, you might know the flood of love and care in those first few days or weeks of their passing. This is showing up, and it is a beautiful gift—the meals, the letters, the phone calls. Four months later, however, as the bereaved are trying to make sense of this new world without their beloved, the loneliness and despair can sink in. Being an ally and friend means also offering support as the work continues and evolves.

I am reminded of the surge of white folks showing up at marches for Black Lives Matter and the attention anti-racist resources received in the months following George Floyd's murder. While this is significant, Black activists and organizers are right to ask if we are actively still working to end systemic racism in our schools, workplaces, and houses of worship. Did the needs and energy of that historic moment lead to a more profound commitment? Or was it all so short-lived? In Paul's words, are we centering "our own interests" or the "interest of others"? Showing up when requested and sticking around builds trust and reflects a genuine sense of solidarity. Guided by a spirit of humility and agility—deferring to others in leadership and tailoring our contributions to their communicated needs and desires—it can make a world of difference during lonely and isolating times. While we may not be able to change the outcome of a complicated situation personally, we can still show up as allies, accompanying our brothers, sisters, and siblings and following their lead.

THE JOY OF PREPARATION

My father-in-law, though retired, will always be an engineer. He has a system for almost everything. When we got our little pop-up camper during the pandemic, I got a window into his preparedness mindset. Weeks before our first camping trip, he texted me to ask if we had started packing yet. "The preparations are half the fun," he affirmed with a smile emoji. In our full weeks of working, parenting, and training our new puppy, we absolutely had not begun packing! I found his joy and excitement so endearing. And honestly, I think about it a lot. There is wisdom here.

Regarding interfaith friendship, I encourage you to lean into my father-in-law's mentality. Embrace your own spiritual formation, the journey of religious literacy, and preparation with a posture of joy. When I speak with Christian seminary students on fire for interfaith engagement, they often ask: *But how do I get started? How do I make inroads?* While this energy heartens me, the image in my mind is that of pumping the breaks. Preparation isn't just necessary, it *is* half the fun—and perhaps more than half the work itself! Learning about other religious and philosophical traditions is something we can each do experientially, as noted in chapter 2, and on our own, with a friend, or in a small faith-sharing group. You might choose to read a series of spiritual autobiographies by folks from other traditions or decide to watch a film each month by a Sikh, Muslim, or Hindu filmmaker. Religious literacy is lifelong work and something that will meaningfully enrich your life. Moreover, preparing your heart for this work will allow you to stay connected to others in your life and to the holy calling you outward. Staying awake to these dimensions of the journey and honoring each step—as you would a walking meditation—will only help you befriend nuance and root you further in courageous humility. Building religious literacy is just one thread of the work, a necessary foundation and a good place to start, but it is not the end.

Another preparation layer would be cultivating and refining your muscles for active listening. Whether at home, work, or school, make a conscious effort to engage those skills. What is it like to take in what your friend, coworker, child, partner, or neighbor says without rushing to add your own two cents? Where might the conversation or relationship go if you offer space, embrace the silence, and listen for what is beneath the words? All of this work is cumulative; it will help shape your day-to-day life with those around you and build the muscles of empathy and compassion.

In her book *Holy Friendships: Nurturing Relationships That Sustain Pastors and Leaders*, Baptist minister and theological educator Victoria Atkinson White invites her readers to be prayerfully proactive. She encourages us to "pray for the friends you have not met yet just as you pray for the ones you already treasure in your life. Share with God the kinds of friends you seek and ask for the Holy Spirit's guidance in finding and connecting with them."[21] I love this simple nudge from Atkinson White. She reminds us that this work is co-creative. God works in the silence and the seemingly empty spaces of our lives. Praying for the opportunity to grow in new directions is a critical step in spiritual formation.

This kind of humility and patience takes me back to Advent, when we cultivate these spiritual gifts to prepare our hearts to receive Jesus. Inhabiting the ethic of active listening and practicing self-emptying, we bring mindfulness and intentionality to this work. With this foundation, we can be fully present with others, engaging genuine curiosity and beginner's mind. Remember that this way of being in the world often leads to a reconfiguring of self. Being open to revelation and conversion requires humility—a sense of deep knowing that we are God's and God's work is ongoing. Think back to Sister Nancy, two years from retirement, and the Holy Spirit practically elbowed her onto a new path of exploration and service. This is lifelong work, indeed.

In his conversation about religious pluralism in Catholic contexts, the late Catholic theologian John Healey used the term *openness to self-redefinition* to capture this posture.[22] Embedded within this framing is that kenotic experience of letting go and allowing the spirit to reshape us. This work is directly at odds with our transactional and individualistic culture. When we are engaged in this "openness," we are not extracting information from those around us; instead, we are entering into a space of possibility and transformation. Our job is to show up, listen, stick around, and be present to the humanity of others—such sensibility and practice of facing outward plants the seeds for new life.

SPIRITUAL PROVOCATION: THE POWER OF SMALL CONNECTIONS—THE EXAMEN

Transformation, conversion, and connection often take root on the smallest of scales in those one-to-one moments, both planned and spontaneous. In chaplaincy, we think of these in-between times as sacred moments—the rich conversations after or before a gathering, or the impromptu check-ins that arise while walking across campus. These interactions are sites worthy of deep theological reflection. In working with students struggling with transitions and in my study of loneliness, I have found that it is not uncommon for folks to discount such moments of connection. While they have their hearts set on seeking a profound/rapturous religious experience of the holy or acquiring an instant community, they often overlook what is before them—the person who also arrives to class ten minutes early, the dining hall workers who always greet them, the dogwalker they see each morning, the person they happened to sit next to at a community dinner who is equally awkward and uncomfortable in the situation.

In my spiritual life, the Examen has helped me stay awake and grow in appreciation of these holy moments—the common, unspectacular everyday sacraments. For me, the Examen has also proved to be an invaluable tool for reckoning with many of the challenging themes of this chapter—the nuances of religious identity, appropriation of tradition, decentering Christianity, unlearning biases, the vital role of kenotic humility in interfaith work, and what it true allyship looks like. Let's first start with an outline of this practice, then I will provide a roadmap for engaging the Examen in this work as well.

There are, of course, many ways to pray the Examen, but when I work with small groups, I often use this accessible format:

1. Pray for God's help. Take a few deep breaths, call your attention to God in your midst, and ask the Holy Spirit to guide you and be present with you during this time. Ask that you may see the day and the world with God's eyes, not just your own.
2. Thanksgiving—give thanks to God for the gift of this day, the gift of your breath, and the countless blessings (small and not-so-small) that unfolded throughout the day. Gratitude is a practice that fosters deep belonging. It is gritty and demanding. This takes practice, but when we see that we are part of something much larger, like a network of life or a nascent community, we can reside in joy and make meaning.
3. Review the day. Start when you woke up and go back through your day. Pay special attention to any strong feelings that come up. As you explore and examine them more deeply, bring attention to whether these feelings brought you closer or further away from God. Another way of phrasing this question is when and where you turned toward God and when and where you turned away from God.
4. Rejoice and seek forgiveness. Lift up and celebrate the ways that brought you closer to God. Then, be honest about the times you fell short, rejecting God's invitation to be in relationship. Thank God for the gift of honesty and the chance to try again.

5. Plant the seeds for tomorrow. Ask God to guide you as you prepare for the new day so you may incorporate these learnings in what is to come. Where do you need help? Don't be afraid to get specific. As you close your time of prayer, take two more deep breaths, calling attention to the breath of life taking up space within your holy body. Remind yourself that each breath you take throughout the day contains the invitation to rest and be in relationship with God. May this proximity bring you comfort.[23]

I invite you to start experimenting with the Examen, just as outlined here, praying during those last ten to fifteen minutes before bed. This practice is often a powerful way to reinforce the foundation of Ignatian Spirituality—finding God in all things. As you gain familiarity with the Examen, I encourage you to consider this modality in your relationships with religious others or anyone different from you. Of course, these feelings might come up naturally in your review of the day, but know that this tool is here to accompany you on your interfaith journey.

Maybe you live in a homogeneous community and do not interact much with folks from other traditions; you can engage the Examen with your small group religious literacy circle or with your reactions to a book or film you have recently enjoyed. Where did you see God? Did you feel your heart expand or constrict? How might you move forward and engage your learnings in the everyday moments in your community?

If you are in a more diverse setting, pay attention to those small moments of encounter—whether at an interfaith gathering or in the grocery store. Were there assumptions you made about this person? How might God invite you into a more generous or actively loving posture? Are there ways you might adore Jesus in the face of others? Are there ways you might show up and stick around to help honor the holy in our brothers, sisters, and siblings? Panning out, can you bring the Examen lens to a local, national, or global issue or event? When you pay close attention to those intense feelings, are you falling back on fear or leaning into a life-giving posture of humility? Of course, these are just a few ideas. The beauty of such spiritual practice is that, guided by the Holy Spirit, you will find your way to enter into this ongoing conversation with God. What a blessing.

A prayer to guide you in this lifelong work.

Always-present God,
help me be present to all who need me.
Help me be present
to those I know too well to actually see
and to those who are unseen strangers to me.
Give me the ability to model your attentiveness, loving gaze
when I view my world,
my family
and my friends,
who are seen and loved by you first.
Finally, may my availability be marked by a desire
to be like your Son:
open to being sent
open to being loved,
open to becoming love in the world.[24]

CHAPTER SIX

Wellspring of Hope
The Sacrament of Interfaith Friendship

In this chapter, I celebrate stories of sacramental breakthrough. These vignettes are instructional and invitational. They highlight noteworthy touch points for interfaith engagement—getting comfortable with being uncomfortable, embracing and expressing hospitality, creating a container to build trust, increasing religious literacy, knowing our limits, and surrendering to the spirit of co-creativity. This list is not a step-by-step process. It is neither exhaustive nor a formula. It is simply an entry point. I have learned so much by reflecting on these moments of connection, and while those learnings will continue, the demands of the present moment will always call us to new paths. The work itself is constantly shifting and changing. Amid all this flux, what we can do is remain present and agile.

The Holy Spirit is right here, our guide and witness—taking in the spontaneous beauty and well-intentioned oversights and missteps. My colleague and friend Elyse says, "This is the work." As I write this on the eve of Holy Week, I feel compelled to remind us that sacraments are gritty. They are complex and multivalent and often come to us through suffering. We only get the Eucharist by the way of the cross, and we are only anointed within the context of physical or spiritual distress. I must honor this reality as we sink deeper into the idea that interfaith friendship is a sacrament. It does not always feel good; it can be intimidating or unsettling. That is okay.

I hope that in reading this book, you have grown to appreciate how messiness can be our best teacher. As a reminder, in the words of my friend Holly, spiritual life isn't about feeling good. It is work, but it is the holiest of work. It is about following a call, connecting to something greater than ourselves, and serving the world. I hope that in sharing these stories, I may inspire you to do the deep reading of *your* already holy life. Where is God breaking in? How have your own experiences across differences—political, religious, ideological—revealed the holy to you? Think back to a school board meeting or a conversation at the food pantry or your community garden; those everyday encounters are doorways to the sacred. I wish you well on your journey of experimenting with and contemplating the richness, joys, and challenges that come from difference. In the meantime, enjoy these stories that offer a taste of sacramental beauty in all its complexity and simplicity.

GETTING COMFORTABLE BEING UNCOMFORTABLE

In October 2021, I attended a sitting hosted by the Tufts Buddhist mindfulness sangha. It was the beginning of the new semester, and I could tell from the energy in the room that students were still in that place of electric discovery—the kind of energy I most associate with autumn and the beginning of an academic year. It was still the height of pandemic precautions, so while we did not shake hands, I excitedly greeted returning students whom I had not seen in person for over a year. Our Buddhist chaplain invited us to sit, and we all found our place.

When I was in divinity school, I visited the Cambridge Zen Center and joined the sangha for sittings on many occasions, but it had been a long time since I had meditated in the community. As I settled on the zafu (meditation cushion), I remembered what it was like to be somewhere new, an outsider engaging in a different practice. My shoulders sank a little lower, but I was keenly aware of the newness, the strangeness. Those early months of returning to in-person gatherings were like a slow reawakening of embodiment. Like that night at Hillel, I had forgotten what it was like to share physical space with others. I forgot what it was like to have that proximity complicated by the genuine distance we may feel when in the presence of another tradition, with its different rituals, symbols, stories, and wisdom. This tension fueled my curiosity.

The pandemic made these experiences and questions fresh, like they had just ripened on the vine. They were juicy and compelling. They were fruits I knew I had tasted before, but the depth of their flavor made me wonder if that was true after all. With this sense of clarity and wonder, I found myself in a place of deep gratitude. I felt connected to students experimenting with different religious and philosophical communities during their first month on campus. *Is this what they are feeling too?* I could only wonder. And I felt connected to the returners, old pros, their hospitality waving folks in. There was no barrier, no pretension. My colleague, the Buddhist chaplain, had set the tone of the space with her signature touch of care and reverence. That soft, metered voice has put many at ease over the years.

Being an outsider that day was an essential experience because crossing the threshold to another kind of practice jolted me awake. After spending many months in the comfort of my house, leading virtual small groups and hosting our online Masses, my body finally remembered what it was like to be along for the ride—to fumble through an exercise in another language—literally and metaphorically. It was a gift to feel connected to these wonderfully awkward parts of myself and the beautiful human beings in this room. While this moment occurred within the crucible of our Interfaith Center, a place like a second home to me and my family, it felt miraculous—a reminder that I should never take for granted the opportunity to inhabit the sacred space of another community. It is, indeed, a precious gift.

The experience of God's grace that evening continues to nourish me. It is this ever-unfolding gift of surprise. I do not earn this grace;

it simply is. The shock of coming to and feeling such a profound connection after months and months of isolation was a balm I didn't know I needed. I had not planned to join the sangha that day for the sitting but had casually accepted the impromptu invitation to join them. How informal moments like that and unsuspecting game-time decisions can yield such profound, transformative experiences will never cease to amaze me. Our God of Surprises hungers for us to be in community, humbled by others, and to have our hearts and religious imaginations stretched. It is about cultivating an internal heart of hospitality—being open to the invitations of others and being willing to let go of our egos, embracing all we do not know.

HOSPITALITY IN ITS MANY FORMS

> "Just hospitality is the practice of God's welcome by reaching out across difference to participate in God's actions, bringing justice and healing in our world of crisis and fear of the ones we call 'other.' To live out God's welcome as just hospitality is a calling and a challenge. As strangers ourselves, and strangers to so many other people, we have the possibility of partnering with others as a sign of God's concern for us all, and for all creation. Hospitality is not the only answer to difference, but it is a challenge to us, pointing us to a future that God intends where riotous difference is welcomed."
>
> —Letty Russell

Several years ago, our then Muslim chaplain, Celene, invited our team for dinner at her house. She lived in New Hampshire, so it felt like a real pilgrimage to make our way to during rush hour traffic! While she was a dear friend I had worked with for several years, I had never seen or experienced her home. When we arrived, she scooped us up with her warmth and hospitality. She had been waiting on the lawn for us to pull up and greeted us with a her arms out wide.

"Welcome to the country," she called to us. She proudly walked us around her garden, delighting in its beauty with us. She knew the space well, but her wonder at it all felt fresh, genuine, and unrehearsed. She, too, was in awe of her backyard and creation. We met her cat, played games with her daughter, and heard endless stories of family. When it came time for dinner, however, I was not prepared. My friend cooked a feast for us, and the dishes kept coming. We sat at her high and extra-long wooden dining room table. The six of us who had traveled from campus, her spouse, child, and mother-in-law. Aromatic stews, fresh vegetables, rice, bread—they were all resting in shallow ornate bowls. And then, as we took in the beauty of all these dishes, my friend returned to the kitchen to bring out the beautiful leftover supper from the night before. "Just in case you would prefer this," she said.

When I think back on this evening, my mind often goes to that moment when she brought out yet another option upon which to feast. There was thoughtfulness, magnanimousness, and practicality. There was more to offer; it might have just been sitting in the refrigerator. Why leave that gift, the potential perfect dish for one of her guests, back in the kitchen? Back in 2020, when we were unable to break bread with others, I contemplated that evening, reminding myself of all the ways Celene expressed hospitality. While the dinner table was the summit, she had received us with such warmth that the experience of hospitality was woven into each moment we were at her home. Her wave to us in the driveway, her joyful presence as we piled out of the car, her garden tour, and the pause at the koi pond so we could all see. She loved this place, and that love was magnified with the opportunity to share with her friends. She gave us a joyful respite. She created a space and atmosphere to share stories and laugh. She laughed with us, at herself, and at the funny family stories that surfaced around the dinner table. She allowed us into the world she and her family had created, this world away from the freneticism of the city.

It would have been easy for us to decline her invitation politely, all of us with our busy lives. But we didn't. Thank goodness for that.

In saying yes to the invitation, we began an adventure leading to a collective experience of radical hospitality. It is a reciprocal thing, the giving and the receiving. More than a statement of "all are welcome," radical hospitality says, "We created this with you in mind." We went back into the kitchen to offer yet another dish. When my colleagues and I were ready to return to the car and head home, our host again acknowledged how long the journey had been to get there. "You won't hit any traffic on the way back," she assured us. This gesture and the invitation helped us see her more clearly—she drove this route twice a day, after all!

While grateful to be able to return to the table with friends and strangers, I do not want to lose the practical wisdom we gained during the pandemic. How might small and not-so-small acts, gestures, and words communicate a spirit of resounding welcome to those around you (and to yourself)? How might you invite others into your world and receive the generosity to share in theirs? What would it look like to cultivate a posture of hospitality as you experience elements of religious and philosophical traditions other than your own?

CREATING A CONTAINER

A few years back, a student named Mandy invited me to dinner. She shared a four-bedroom apartment with five other senior students at Tufts. These women were from diverse backgrounds—racially, ethnically, and religiously. They studied in different fields but found their common ground in gathering around the supper table once a week. When I had the great privilege of being their guest, I brought fixings for a salad. "Wow, fresh vegetables!" they screamed, with only some irony. We plated the salad beside heaping helpings of delicious pasta and homemade sauce and feasted together in that small upstairs kitchen.

Mandy was a fierce feminist and a writer, and she was also the president of the Catholic Community at Tufts. As she once articulated in a Q&A with a guest speaker, "I feel like I am often too religious for my feminist friends and too feminist for my religious friends." Mandy lived in the in-betweenness of her identities, which, for her and many Catholic feminists, are complementary and not incongruous. As we sat at the supper table that night, I saw how the wisdom of the table brought together these young folks who were learning deeply from one another. They asked questions of genuine curiosity. They graciously took up space and were agile when others pushed back. There was confidence, and composure at that table, which truly inspired me. Several of them were suspicious of my presence—and rightfully so. What would it mean to have a chaplain at their apartment? And yet, they welcomed me in. While these women might not have the opportunity to live close to one another—and so many peers—later in life, they used their time on campus to enrich themselves and learn about those different from them. In so doing, they also worked out the muscles of intimacy and vulnerability.

I often heard about these dinner table conversations on Sunday nights while cleaning up after Mass with Mandy. It was clear that these women had added a whole new dimension to her life and spiritual journey. The integrity of the space and the authentic process of inner exploration brought them to a place of mutual relation. Their apartment was a container for these conversations—physically and metaphorically. The deep trust I heard over supper that night revealed that they were operating with a scaffolding, a structure to hold them in moments of disagreement. Such spaces take time and patience to create. They grow in the micro-movements of a walk home or making coffee, still bleary-eyed. In addition to trust, building a container for dialogue around difference requires attentiveness and care. An experience in our Interfaith Student Council (ISC) might help bring that value into focus.

The ISC is a community of representatives from different religious and philosophical student groups at Tufts. We meet weekly over dinner, and through storytelling and shared spiritual practice, we seek to build relationships, grow in religious literacy, and envision programmatic offerings for the broader campus. Given the pace of life on campus and the demands placed on each of these student leaders within their respective communities, we also envision our time together as a space of renewal, rest, and joy.

A few years ago, I had the gift of co-facilitating the ISC with our chaplaincy intern, Fran. When we returned from winter break, we wanted to create a space for students to share from the particularity of their observance. Fran introduced me to the term *heartifact* and suggested inviting the team to bring a physical object that spoke to their spiritual, religious, philosophical, or personal journey. They were to show it to the group and then share why it was meaningful. At first, the term *heartifact* felt overly precious, like nerdy seminary-speak, but slowly, it grew on me, and we embraced it. We sat around the wooden table when the students arrived and started our usual check-in process. Fran read Pablo Neruda's poem, "Ode to Things," as a centering practice. She explained that each student was to share their heartifact one by one. The students listening would be employing their active listening skills. After each person was done sharing, they would say, "I have spoken," to which the group would respond, "We have listened." After a period of pause, the listeners would be able to ask just three questions. In ritualizing the process, we aimed to focus on the spirit of generosity and hospitality of heart. Moreover, in a group that is often high-spirited and prone to chatting incessantly, we needed to formalize this space to reflect the significance of these gifts.

Several students shared something special they wore each day on their person—a Saint Christopher's medal, a Star of David. Our representative from the Hindu community shared his kautuka, the red thread on his wrist that his mother fastened to him each time he left for the semester—a ritual symbol of protection. We heard a story of jewelry lost at summer camp and the internal discernment process as they tried to decide what to choose.

One student had forgotten about the "homework" and, during our check-in, he combed through his backpack, looking for something to present. He ended up sharing his TI-95 calculator. He was not a math major or engineer; he did not like those courses at all, but this machine had been with him since the eighth grade. He was bashful sharing about his calculator, embarrassed that he hadn't prepared with more intention, but it was a beautiful example of doing the deep reading of our lives and finding God in all things. As he went on, he surprised himself with how much he had to say! This machine had an origin story. It had walked with him through challenging times in high school, paving the way for his college experience. Then he told us about the notes of encouragement he used to write in the calculator. He would open the notes section during exams and find strength and inspiration from his pep talk to himself! This tender practice moved many of his classmates, their compassion audible in ohs and aws.

A Muslim student shared the prayer rug his mother had brought back for him when she visited her home country. With deep care and delight, he raised the rug in the light and showed us the delicate gold thread that outlined the calligraphy and how this style differed from those more common in the United States. This connection to his mom and a home he knew in his bones meant so much to him. An Orthodox Christian student brought an icon gifted to her on her way to college, and a Catholic student brought his Greek New Testament, something he purchased in Greece after a transformative experience learning about the Orthodox Church.

While these were powerful moments of generosity and vulnerability, the beauty of each share was magnified by the care, wonder, and genuine curiosity expressed in the three questions. Upon the "I have spoken" and "We have listened" call and response, the group held the moment with a longer pause. And then the questions would begin. They were careful with their words. They did not rush into asking but took a moment, knowing it would be one less question for the group if they jumped to ask something casual. As listeners, the exercise encouraged them to honor those around them. Slowly and with deep care, they asked clarifying questions about tradition and meaning. They asked more personal questions about what it meant to the sharer: *Did it remind them of a story or a family member? Is there a reason you always wear your necklace beneath your clothing? Does the significance change as the color fades? Where do you keep it when you are not using it?*

As I reflected more on the substance of the evening, I marveled at what brought us to that moment—a foundation of trust, empathy, and friendship. We had been meeting as a community for five months, sharing a mid-week meal and building foundational connections in one-on-ones and small groups. It takes time to build trust. It takes sharing stories and chatting over meals. It takes being in one another's presence and getting to know the hearts in the room. I have found that in interfaith spaces, the more the foundation is tended to, the greater depth we can go when the time comes—whether in rich moments like this or, sadly, in times of acute crisis. The foundation holds us, and when times get tough, and a disagreement ensues—as it indeed will—knowing the hearts in the room is lifesaving. I may not agree with everyone at the table, politically or theologically. Still, I know that they are loving human beings who, like me, are working hard to find their way, support their families, and be considerate community members.

RELIGIOUS LITERACY

Ali and Peter were roommates for four years at Tufts University. They had been paired by the residential life matching method as incoming students and instantly hit it off. Both men were deeply religious—Peter, a Catholic, and Ali, a Muslim. These young men, named by their parents with wonderfully iconic names from their respective traditions, often found that they had more in common than they did with students from their student religious organizations. They were deeply invested in one another's lives and families. During their shifts working at the Interfaith Center and the Chapel, Ali and Peter would tell us about the long conversations they had at night. They shared the stories of their immigrant families, spiritual practices, and the central elements of their respective traditions.

One evening, as they lay in their beds, Peter elaborated on his Italian family's devotion to Mary. He talked about the art on his grandmother's walls and his practice of praying the rosary. "She is our mother," he said. "She holds all of our sorrow and joy." To his great surprise, Ali began to expound on the role of Maryam (Mary) in Islam. Peter was floored. He had no idea that Maryam appeared in the Qur'an and that Muslims upheld her virginity. Similarly, Ali was keen to learn how personal and meaningful Mary was to Peter. Their connection over Mary/Maryam—this shared, celebrated figure from their traditions—inspired the young men to host an afternoon gathering for Catholic and Muslim students to tell stories and go deeper.

The story of Ali and Peter shows the sacramental power of creating a sacred space and the transformative act of listening. While the dorm room was ordinary in its function, it became a sacred space, a site of beholding as the holy broke in—inhabiting the space between these two friends. Their spiritual journeys intersected and twisted around one another as they listened with attentiveness and genuine curiosity. The friendship of Ali and Peter teaches us how dyadic connectedness affects the greater whole. The ripples of their friendship continue to be felt even after graduation. Students spoke of this Mary/Maryam conversation long after they were gone, even those who were unable to attend that day and were not yet enrolled at Tufts!

During their program, Peter and Ali talked about the cost of loneliness: that it is not simply the inner pain of the isolated individual but all that fails to enter the community due to disconnection. From the Catholic lens, it is the Body of Christ that suffers. Each part is necessary (1 Cor. 12:22, NRSV). To think, all those moments of potential connection that could have been lost—the dismantling of anti-Muslim bias, the expansion of religious literacy, the sense of wonder around discovering and rediscovering elements of one's tradition. In this way, the relationship between these two young men captures Mary Hunt's vision for friendships breaking down walls of oppression and prejudice.

The Mary/Maryam program reverberates into the landscape of trinitarian theology. From my Catholic lens, I imagine their dorm room conversations as witnessed and inspired by the Holy Spirit. As historian James McEvoy puts it, friendship is a mystery of God's grace, which is "the origin of friendship between parties who do not at the very outset resemble each other but through 'the Spirit of

God's working redemption within their souls,'" come to find deep resonance and recognition with each other.[1] It brought these two men into a place of spiritual boldness and transformative vulnerability. On another level, however, the foundational element of the Trinity is difference. The Triune God lifts up the holiness of diversity and testifies to a more profound unity in multiplicity. Difference is holy. Moreover, it bears notice that Peter and Ali united to honor Mary/Maryam in all *her* complexity. They wished to shed light on the differences to understand her better. She was not merely a medium through which to get to God; they held her story and the stories of their traditions as holy. This kind of nuance is countercultural. It rejects the essentialization of such a critical character and instead draws out a deep desire for something authentic and relatable.

There are so many things to love about this story, but I sincerely appreciate the movement from a one-to-one friendship to a community offering. Ali and Peter had the natural impulse to share what they had learned. This came from a place of deep joy, but we should be keen to learn from them and their outward-facing posture. Brother John of Taizé writes, "Modern society has privatized friendship, turning it into a predominantly emotional and individual reality. Christians must 'de-privatize friendship,' rediscovering its public character."[2] I believe in the transformative power of the one-to-one. Still, because of our culture of individualism and loneliness, we must be careful not to keep these gifts hidden under the proverbial bushel basket. Several of the stories in this chapter celebrate the beauty and power of a community-centered lens. Yes, we are to gain wisdom and understanding from one another. Still, I hope we can turn toward the collective and share the gift of religious literacy, active listening, and empathy building with the broader community landscape.

KNOWING ONE'S LIMITS

One spring afternoon, I had tea with Anna, an alumna who sings in our choir. She updated me about spiritual life after graduation and the big questions on her heart as a young professional. Then she told me a story. When the lockdown began, she found herself hungry for connection. Everyone was so isolated, and she needed to get a "spiritual itch scratched." A former coworker had invited her to join a dharma talk hosted by friends from her sangha. The first time she attended, they went deep fast. They talked about purpose and meaning. When the conversation shifted to questions of right action and wrong action, Anna was asked to share in a breakout room, and she connected it to her concept of sin. The folks on the call were genuinely interested—"Tell us more about that," they said. As she looked back on that experience, Anna reported feeling energized by the conversation. It was enriching and inspired her to think more deeply about her tradition. When her friend invited her to the next session, Anna was pleased to accept.

At that next gathering, however, something shifted. The group transitioned to meditative practice and recitation when the dharma talk ended. She was excited to experiment with the meditation, but she felt unsettled when the recitation (chanting) began.

"It didn't feel right," she said, smiling and shaking her head. And then, putting herself back into the moment, she impersonated herself: "No, no, no I don't think I'll do that." I was transfixed by her narration of that moment of dis-ease. I had not seen it coming and was grateful for her honesty. When I asked her to unpack her distress, she got quiet. "I don't fully know. I was worried about being disrespectful. Was it an insult not to participate? But I thought about what it means when we chant together in Mass. We are reciting the creed or saying prayers. I didn't know the words in that virtual gathering because they were in another language. How could I say something if I didn't know what it meant?"[3]

It was a year and a half later when Anna and I sat on that patio drinking tea, and I was moved by the care with which she had held this memory. "This means something to me," she told me, "the whole thing brought me to a new awareness of what it means to speak in unison. I think of the novenas I pray with my family and how powerful it is to say something together. The next time I was at Mass,

I heard the creed in a new way." Her smile widened, and her voice lifted. "I realized, 'Wait, I really do believe this.'" I heard such freshness and elation in Anna's voice. The experience brought her closer to her faith and sharpened her perspective on a practice that had become so familiar its significance had been dulled.

Anna was able to name the exact moment of challenge and had done the reflection necessary to understand where it was coming from. This brought her to a place of clarity around her Catholic observance, and she drew strength and conviction from her insights. We always experience other traditions through our own lens, but Anna shows us how to do so with a generous heart and attention to our boundaries. When she logged on, was she expecting the meditation session to lead to a reflection on what it means for her to recite the creed each week? I suspect not. One of the beautiful realities of interfaith friendship and engagement is how they often open doorways to encountering (or re-encountering) one's tradition. When we have hosted interfaith Masses or teaching Masses, I have found that Catholic students learn just as much or more than their visiting peers! These entry points allow us to renew the soil of our spiritual lives, overturning that richness, breaking up the layers on the surface, and getting to the nutrients beneath.

REVELATORY EXPERIENCING

On any given day on a college campus, dozens of events are happening. As part of the multifaith chaplaincy at Tufts University, we coordinate our offerings to avoid overlap or conflicts. We value a collaborative spirit, and we want students to attend the gatherings of other groups. Last fall, at the beginning of the term, we found ourselves in a position where several events were planned for the same Friday. The Interfaith Student Council discovered this mishap as we began our sacred calendaring process. At that point, it was too late to make any significant changes date-wise. However, I embraced this blunder as an opportunity to illustrate the deep value of communication and being in sync.

Earlier in the semester, Fran had teasingly used the term "sacred calendaring." I took a shine to it immediately. As two theo-nerds, we started unpacking the phrase and found that it got to the heart of what we hoped to do. What are the seasons in our lives? How do we keep track of time? How do our traditions keep track of time? Whether throughout the day, pausing to pray, or the many feasts/holidays/celebrations connected to the lunar calendar or the liturgical calendars. And what about the impact of the academic calendar on our spiritual lives? We wanted to honor the act of sharing and teaching about our traditions as sacred and hopefully move toward cocreating a living, breathing calendar that would witness religious and philosophical life on campus and encourage participation across traditions.

The evening began as usual, with Fran laying out the dinner from a local take-out joint. After our check-in and grounding practice, we jumped into the task. In freehand-drawn columns, Fran had mapped out the rest of the semester on the whiteboard—week by week. We asked for a volunteer, and Paul, our representative from the Protestant community, quickly raised his hand. He had a plan of color-coded events, but that didn't last long. The students at the table behind him yelled out dates in between bites of falafel.

"We are doing interfaith ghost stories at Hillel next Thursday at two thirty, and then first-year Shabbat is Friday at six p.m.," said Aviva, getting us started.

"Woah, say more about that, ghost stories?" yelled Kaisa from the other side of the room. Then she turned to the board and added, "Death Café is this Friday at seven, and you all need to come; it's going to be sick."

"In Living Memory is next Thursday at eight in the chapel," said Ari from the Interfaith Ambassadors.

"And the meeting about climate grief is next Wednesday at eight," added Joanna, "which is different. We usually meet on Mondays."

Sitting right next to Paul, Ahmed added, "November twelfth is Muslim Student Association Fall Dinner. Everyone's invited."

"Don't forget the In Living Memory Decoration party on Monday night. You're all invited to help. There will be pizza, and we are making lanterns," added Ari. Paul drew an arrow connecting the decoration party at five on Monday night and the eight o'clock evening event three days later on Thursday. He was going as quickly as possible, but it was hard to keep up. And the dates kept coming!

"All Saints' Day Mass is November first," said Erin, "and we have a community dinner every first Sunday of the month, so the next one's coming up."

"And we are celebrating Diwali this Friday at six," said Saagar.

By now, Paul, in his six-three frame, was crouched on the floor to reach the bottom of the whiteboard. He kept going, but the process had clearly entered a new stage of absurdity as we saw just how nonlinear our calendar had become. Some of the events at the top of the week occurred on Friday, and Monday's gatherings were at the bottom of the following week because there was no more room.

Fran and I looked at each other with wide eyes. We were taking it in. This beautiful mess of human beings, their voices and personalities, had become something else altogether. The shouting of dates and the running commentary of side conversations—when was the first documented Golem story, and why do they serve cake at Death Café? The shock of what was happening as it was happening had brought the energy in the seminar room to a new level. Just a few short weeks before, this group of thirteen student leaders had gathered for our first evening, and there had been some trepidation and curiosity around what it would look like to surrender an hour and a half each week to the council. Later in the year, I would learn how uneasy some students were with the idea. Were we going to be hanging out in robes, reciting scripture? Were they going to have to go on trial defending their tradition or be some kind of expert?[4] What I saw that October evening, however, was the beginning of deep connection. The vulnerability, the rawness, the joy, the playfulness, the rowdiness. It was thrilling to behold. Would it be fruitful if every meeting was this boisterous? No. But its rarity was what made it so memorable and rich.

As the dates slowed down, Ari and Joanna decided this was a job for a shared electronic document, and they graciously took the initiative to create it. Paul went on to transcribe the only two events on the calendar for finals in December, and the room grew quiet. The students took a step back with pride.

"Wow," I heard someone say, "that is so cool. Just look at all we are doing to support spiritual life on campus." There was something powerful in magnifying the beauty of that already around us—beholding, enjoying, delighting in.

As the energy in the room shifted into a more reflective space, another student added, "I'm glad we didn't begin with the computer. If I had just added my community's events, I would haven't been paying attention to everything you all are doing."

"And it definitely wouldn't have been as much fun," added Erin, with a wry smile.

That was undoubtedly true.

That evening, we planted seeds for co-creative and spontaneous learning. Would we have arrived at this fruitful place of shared journey and exploration without the wonderful mess of our sacred calendaring experiment? Maybe in due time, but certainly not as quickly as we did. The spirit of spontaneity from that night nourished the underlying threads within this council, fast-tracking them to a place of ownership and meaningful connection. At the end of the semester, we closed the last meeting by inviting everyone to share one thing they would take with them over the break—a memory, an insight, anything. Many students said they were going to take the sacred calendaring with them. I silently thought to myself: They, too, felt it! The transformation, the beauty, and the absurdity. A holy night indeed.

In her book *The Grace of Playing*, practical theologian Courtney Goto uses the term *revelatory experiencing* when describing events like our sacred calendaring. This phrase points toward movement and dynamism. It is not located in a single experience, which might suggest one could reach a climax or endpoint; instead, she is concerned with the ever-unfolding nature of living with this kind of posture or intentionality. She is concerned with the process of living, learning, and cocreating. Goto writes, "Revelatory experiencing is more personal, compelling, and uncanny than other learning. It often addresses what is needed in the moment for more abundant living and what cannot be sought directly because it was not previously known."[5]

When I think back on that evening and those moments of awe as I tried to understand the energy in that room, I see that I was part of a shared revelatory experience within this community of student leaders. I could have never imagined the fruitfulness of watching the board fill with that jumble of dates and then the slow disentangling of that nonlinearity that was eventually tackled on the spreadsheet. But by then, we were changed. We had built something together that was drawn from the core of our communities and values, and we laughed so hard at the absurdity—all while spontaneous religious literacy took place between neighbors and even those sitting on opposite sides of the room. Remember the Golem question? That conversation continued later that evening as students reflected on what counts as an origin story—can we ever really know when a story begins?

For Goto, this is all part of revelatory experiencing—decentering and re-centering. She writes, "Revelatory experiencing causes in learners a destabilizing and re-orienting shift in awareness or feeling that allows them to encounter divine mystery, themselves, and others in new, life-giving ways."[6] As I reflect on my memory of that evening, I am reminded of the casual comments I heard from quiet students and watching in delightful awe as once-hidden aspects of their personalities rose to the surface—playful remarks in good taste but with elements of sarcasm or unexpected sharpness. There was a candidness to those words, revealing a side of personality they had held closer to their chest in the earlier weeks of our time together. I welcomed this fuller picture of them. Our multidimensional identities are never fully knowable, but it is a gift to be reminded that there is always so much more beneath the surface.

Goto's framework of revelatory experience describes this landmark moment in our community's formation. Still, in the introduction of her text, she is quick to say that "the more one attempts to parse what is going on in revelatory experiencing, the more the embodied memory and wonder of translucence seems to dissipate . . . any description of revelatory experiencing is inherently vague, like telling someone who has never seen snow what it is like to ski."[7] I take deep comfort in this passage, as it relieves me of the burden of trying to put into language that which is inherently ineffable. It was a "you simply had to be there" kind of story. Still, it invites us to honor the vital role of play and joy in transformative interfaith work. Christians do not always value the playfulness of the Holy Spirit, which is hard to understand. Many of Jesus's parables are steeped in humor and even absurdity. Have you ever imagined a tree trunk sticking out of your eye? Moreover, the image of Jonah and the whale is widely beloved, but what is that story if it is not an epic game of hide and seek? Our tradition is chock-full of playfulness, but many of us have been conditioned to think of religion as only serious business. This limits our imagination and capacity to innovate.

As you embrace the work of building interfaith friendships, I invite you to sit with Goto's call to destabilize and reorient. It takes humility and courage to do this work, but we will find our guide by trusting in the spirit. This is no formula for developing interfaith friendships, but what follows are a few suggestions so you can prepare yourself to step into new spaces of creativity and welcome revelatory experiences when they arise.

1. Do your homework. While interfaith engagement goes well beyond learning the basics of other religious and philosophical traditions, religious literacy is necessary. In the appendix, you will find a list of a few books to help you get started. Keep in mind that even the term *religion* is a construct. That means we may bring biases into what we consider traditions worthy of study. For instance, when I first started in chaplaincy, there was conversation around

whether atheists or nonreligious folks (Nones) should even be included at the table. These days, this question is hardly entertained, as we know the deep value that such folks bring to the community. There are also folks whose observance and tradition might not fall into the typical notion of religion or who might not resonate with the label *religion*. I am thinking especially of Indigenous communities who have raised the concern that the term *religion* is yet another colonial framework that does not capture the essence of their identity and culture.

2. Learn your community. Go deep. Is there an interfaith organization within your city or town? Is there a coalition that does religious/philosophical advocacy for social justice? If so, reach out, attend their meetings or community actions, and . . . listen. Listen. Listen. Listen. What are the questions that they are wrestling with? Who is leading/speaking? How might you support and magnify the good work already being done? Stay awake to those around you, but also be aware of your biases or when you find yourself experiencing moments of discomfort or tension. Find someone to help you unpack your baggage and unlearn any dangerous thinking and theology that has infected you.

3. Be patient. Remember that you are playing the long game. Building meaningful connections takes time and patience. We must move at the speed of trust. If you are excited to get started, that's wonderful and quite natural, honestly. The challenge will be to keep your enthusiasm in check so you can be present and observant in a respectful and conscientious manner. Again, use those active listening skills—they will help you gain a deeper understanding of both the outer landscape and your own inner landscape.

4. Work out your agility muscles. We have to be ready to shift and pivot and to continue holding it all with deep care. The Holy Spirit is constantly guiding us in new, unfamiliar directions—trust in the Spirit's work. This posture might

be a challenge for many, especially those steeped in tradition who find comfort in rigidity. This kind of spiritual sensibility can be cultivated.
5. Be aware of your positionality and how it affects your relationship to power and privilege. Humility and courage will guide you as you unpack your identities. It is in our particularity that we can go deep and plunge the depths of connection and tradition. There may be anxiety and fear around change, difference, and holding these tensions simultaneously. I invite you to acknowledge that fear and get curious about it so you might understand where it is coming from.
6. Be prepared for tension. After all, in the words of my friend and mentor Jenny, meaningful engagement with difference will result in "divergent perspectives." That is okay. In fact, that is the work! Trust in those active listening skills to guide you. How might they help you hear those around you and also your own internal monologue? Bring that spirit of genuine curiosity with you.
7. Beginner's mind. I join you in the lifelong work of cultivating an orientation toward learning. In the spirit of Richard Rohr, that includes the forever learning of the Holy Trinity and the sacraments, as well as the world around us. Befriending humility, wonder, and openness is a great first step.
8. Be open to being changed.

Notes

INTRODUCTION

1 Anantanand Rambachan, "'Love Speaking to Love:' Friendship Across Religious Traditions," in *Friendship Across Religions: Theological Perspectives on Interreligious Friendship*, ed. Alon Goshen-Gottstein (New York: Lexington Books, 2015), 110.

CHAPTER ONE: FRIENDSHIP IN THE TRADITION

1 John 11:27.
2 Nathan C. Johnson, "When Seventy Equals Seventy-Two: A Reception-Historical Contribution to the Text-Critical Problem of Luke 10:1, 17," *Journal of Theological Studies* 70, no. 2 (July 2019): 650, https://doi.org/10.1093/jts/flz084.
3 Luke 24:13–25.
4 Nora Chadwick, *The Age of the Saints in the Early Celtic Church* (London: Oxford University Press, 1961), 103.
5 For an account of John Cassian's life and writings, see Columba Stewart, *Cassian the Monk*, Oxford Studies in Historical Theology (Oxford: Oxford University Press, 1998).
6 William Harmless, *Desert Christians: An Introduction to the Literature of Early Monasticism* (London: Oxford University Press, 2004), 417. Harmless rejects the oversimplified narrative of monasticism's origin story. His chapter "Monastic Origins: Perspectives, Discoveries, and Disputed Questions" goes deep into the different geographical and cultural contexts of Egypt, Syria, Cappadocia, and Palestine. He lifts up current scholarly work that acknowledges the agendas of church historians and what scholars have learned from the archeological and papyrological lenses.
7 "Like most ancients, Cassian was uneasy about novelty; he, like them, believed that new was bad and old was good. And he was concerned to show that monastics, far from being some newfangled fourth-century invention,

was Christianity's oldest and most faithful remnant." Harmless, *Desert Christians*, 417–418.
8   Edward C. Sellner, *Stories of the Celtic Soul Friends: Their Meaning for Today* (New York: Paulist, 2004), 45.
9   Sellner, *Stories of the Celtic Soul Friends*, 44.
10 Laura Swan, *The Forgotten Desert Mothers: Sayings, Lives, and Stories of Early Christian Women* (New York: Paulist, 2001), 17.
11 Swan, *The Forgotten Desert Mothers*, 10.
12 Christine Valters Paintner, "The Desert Mothers and Fathers Showed Us All Life Is Sacred: Experience God in Every Moment," *US Catholic* 85, no. 2 (January 31, 2020): 20–23.
13 Chadwick, *The Age of the Saints in the Early Celtic Church*, 103.
14 Sellner, *Stories of the Celtic Soul Friends*, 94.
15 Ray Simpson, *Soul Friendship in the Celtic Tradition: Ancient Insights for Today* (Vestal, NY: Anamchara Books, 2021), 181.
16 John O'Donohue, *Anam Cara: A Book of Celtic Wisdom* (New York: HarperCollins, 1997), 32.
17 Cited by Liz Carmichael, *Friendship: Interpreting Christian Love* (London: T&T Clark, 2004), 48.
18 Carmichael, *Friendship*, 71.
19 Aelred of Rievaulx, *Spiritual Friendship*, ed. Marsha L. Dutton, trans. Lawrence C. Braceland (Collegeville, MN: Cistercian, 2010), 72–73 (italics editor's).
20 Aelred, *Spiritual Friendship*, 126.
21 Taken into the practical context of ministry and service, I think of a dear colleague of mine who has reflected deeply on Eucharistic Adoration in action. Her practice of Adoration takes place on the sidewalk, out in the streets, serving those most in need. She asks: If we only adore Christ in the sanctuary, in a defined liturgical space, are we embracing the spirit of Jesus's message?
22 William A. Barry, *A Friendship Like No Other: Experiencing God's Amazing Embrace* (Chicago: Loyola, 2008), 108.
23 John of Taizé, *Friends in Christ: Paths to a New Understanding of Church* (Maryknoll, NY: Orbis Books, 2012), 128.
24 Barry, *A Friendship Like No Other*, 95.
25 Thomas Merton, *Thoughts in Solitude* (New York: Farrar, Straus & Giroux, 1958), 79.
26 John, *Friends in Christ*, 128.

CHAPTER TWO: INTERDEPENDENCE AND DIFFERENCE

1   Leonardo Boff, *Holy Trinity, Perfect Community*, trans. Phillip Berryman (Maryknoll, NY: Orbis Books, 2000), 123.
2   Boff, *Holy Trinity, Perfect Community*, 17.

3   Elizabeth A. Johnson, *She Who Is: The Mystery of God in Feminist Theological Discourse* (Chestnut Ridge, NY: Crossroad, 1992), 222.
4   Tertullian, "De Corona Militis," trans. S. Thelwell, from *Ante-Nicene Fathers* vol. 3, *Tertullian*, ed. Alexander Roberts, James Donaldson, and A. Cleveland Coxe, revised and edited for *New Advent* by Kevin Knight (Buffalo, NY: Christian Literature Publishing, 1885), https://www.newadvent.org/fathers/0304.htm.
5   Richard Rohr, *The Divine Dance: The Trinity and Your Transformation* (New Kensington, PA: Whitaker House, 2016), 27 (my italics).
6   Catherine Mowry LaCugna, *God for Us: The Trinity and Christian Life* (New York: HarperCollins, 1991), 269.
7   LaCugna, *God for Us*, 272.
8   Carter Heyward, *Saving Jesus from Those Who Are Right: Rethinking What It Means to Be Christian* (Minneapolis, MN: Fortress Press, 1999), 73.
9   LaCugna, *God for Us*, 334.
10 LaCugna, *God for Us*, 321.
11 LaCugna, *God for Us*, 321.
12 Catherine Mowry LaCugna, "The Practical Trinity," *The Christian Century* 109 no. 2 (July 15–22, 1992): 681.
13 LaCugna, *God for Us*, 321–22. LaCugna's use of the term *economy* pertains to her greater thesis around the economics of the Trinity and the need to understand the Trinity in terms of salvation.
14 Mary Elizabeth Mullino Moore, *Teaching as a Sacramental Act* (Cleveland, OH: Pilgrim, 2004), 10. Moore unpacks the loaded moments of connection wherein the holy breaks through. She approaches sacramental theology from the lens of her vocation as a teacher, but her attention to consciousness-building around sacramental imagination is something I will continue to return to. Moore defines sacraments as "the conveyance of God's grace through signs in creation for the sanctification of human beings and the well-being of all God's creation." Her definition bears dynamism and movement. As a Catholic hoping to inspire a more creative sacramental consciousness in Catholic students, I find her definition invigorating. It draws upon much the same language and communicates the same essence, but it is free of the stock phrases that desensitize us to the radical, profound, and ubiquitous nature of sacraments.
15 Roberto Catalano, "The Role of Ecclesial Movements in the Implementation of *Nostra Aetate*," in *Catholicism Engaging Other Faiths: Vatican II and its Impact*, ed. Vladimir Latinovic, Gerard Mannion, and Jason Welle (Cham, Switzerland: Palgrave Macmillan, 2018), 79.
16 "This document, therefore, is proposed in order to help Christian communities and especially their leaders to live according to the directives of the Council," Secretariat for Non-Christians; "The Attitude of the Church Towards the Followers of Other Religions: Reflections and Orientations on Dialogue and Mission," address of the Pope (Vatican City, March 3, 1984).

NOTES

17 Michael Fitzgerald and John Borelli, *Interfaith Dialogue: A Catholic View* (Maryknoll, NY: Orbis Books, 2010), 390.
18 Joan Chittister, *The Liturgical Year: The Spiraling Adventure of the Spiritual Life*, The Ancient Practices Series, (Nashville, TN: Thomas Nelson, 2009), 183.
19 Thích Nhất Hạnh, "The Insight of Interbeing," in *The Art of Living* (New York: HarperOne, 2017).

CHAPTER THREE: LISTENING TO GOD, OURSELVES, AND ONE ANOTHER

1 Known as the *we-passages* (Acts 16:10–17, 20:5–15, 21:1–18, 27:1–28:16), this section differs from the previous fifteen chapters. Scholars continue to debate whether this shift is a stylistic decision, an example of interpolation (a later edit), or an attempt to create the illusion that the author was a direct eyewitness. Our job here is not to get to the bottom of this scriptural debate but to honor and explore the significance of the "we."
2 Eric Barreto, "Commentary on Acts 16:9–15," *Working Preacher* (blog), Luther Seminary, May 9, 2010, https://www.workingpreacher.org/commentaries/revised-common-lectionary/sixth-sunday-of-easter-3/commentary-on-acts-169-15-2.
3 "Tyrian Purple," *Origins of Color* exhibition, University of Chicago Library, April 16, 2007, https://www.lib.uchicago.edu/collex/exhibits/originsof-color/organic-dyes-and-lakes/tyrian-purple.
4 "Tyrian Purple."
5 Pope Francis, "Pope Calls for a 'Listening Church,'" address at commemorative ceremony for the fiftieth anniversary of the Synod of Bishops, trans. Thomas Rosica, October 17, 2015, https://www.americamagazine.org/content/all-things/pope-calls-listening-church.
6 Carl R. Rogers and Richard E. Farson, *Active Listening* (Mansfield Centre, CT: Martino, 2015).
7 Rogers and Farson, *Active Listening*.
8 Kevin O'Brien, *The Ignatian Adventure: Experiencing the Spiritual Exercises of Saint Ignatius in Daily Life* (Chicago: Loyola, 2011), 53.
9 Carl McColman, *The Big Book of Christian Mysticism: The Essential Guide to Contemplative Spirituality* (San Francisco: Hampton Roads, 2010), 224.
10 Sherry Turkle, *Reclaiming Conversation: The Power of Talk in a Digital Age* (New York: Penguin, 2015), 213.
11 Turkle, *Reclaiming Conversation*, 213.
12 Carl McColman, *Befriending Silence: Discovering the Gifts of Cistercian Spirituality* (Notre Dame, IN: Ave Maria, 2015), 11.
13 Shunryu Suzuki, *Zen Mind, Beginner's Mind: Informal Talks on Zen Meditation and Practice* (New York: Weatherhill, 1980), 21.
14 Matt 18:1.
15 Matt 18:2–5.

16 Judith Jones, "Commentary on Matthew 18:1–9," *Working Preacher* (blog), Luther Seminary, February 22, 2023, https://www.workingpreacher.org/commentaries/narrative-lectionary/who-is-the-greatest-2/commentary-on-matthew-181-9-3.

CHAPTER FOUR: SACRAMENTAL CONSCIOUSNESS AND PARTICIPATION

1 Hosffman Ospino, "No Synodal Church Without Catechetical Reform," lecture, Gloria L. and Charles I. Clough School of Theology and Ministry at Boston College, October 12, 2023, Brighton, MA, https://www.bc.edu/content/bc-web/schools/stm/sites/encore/main/2023/no-synodal-church-without-catechetical-reform.html.
2 Ospino, "No Synodal Church."
3 John F. Baldovin and David Farina Turnbloom, "Catholics: A Sacramental People" in *Catholic Sacraments: A Rich Source of Blessings* (New York: Paulist, 2015), 5.
4 Rohr, *The Divine Dance*, 27 (my italics).
5 Kathleen Hughes, *Becoming the Sign: Sacramental Living in a Post-Conciliar Church* (New York: Paulist, 2013), 40.
6 Leonardo Boff, *Sacraments of Life: Life of the Sacraments*, trans. John Drury (Portland, OR: Pastoral Press, 1987), 16.
7 Boff, 7–8.
8 Andrew M. Greeley, *The Catholic Imagination* (Berkeley: University of California Press, 2000), 1.
9 Mary Hunt, *Fierce Tenderness: A Feminist Theology of Friendship* (Chestnut Ridge, NY: Crossroad, 1992), 117.
10 Andre Dubus, "Sacraments," in *Signatures of Grace: Catholic Writers on the Sacraments*, ed. Thomas Grady and Paula Huston (Eugene, OR: Wipf & Stock, 2001), 222.
11 Dubus, 220.
12 Pope Francis, *Evanglii Gaudium*, Vatican City, November 24, 2013, paragraph 120, https://www.vatican.va/content/francesco/en/apost_exhortations/documents/papa-francesco_esortazione-ap_20131124_evangelii-gaudium.html.
13 Nadia Bolz-Weber, "Day 3 Mass Gathering" (event recording), Evangelical Lutheran Church in America, June 29, 2018, https://www.youtube.com/watch?v=YBtyZbauH0g.
14 Pope Francis, *Address at the Opening of the Synod of Bishops on Young People, the Faith and Vocational Discernment*, Rome, October 3, 2018 (italics original), https://www.vatican.va/content/francesco/en/speeches/2018/october/documents/papa-francesco_20181003_apertura-sinodo.html.
15 Vatican Council II, *Decree on the Apostolate of the Laity*, Apostolicam Actuositatem, promulgated by Pope Paul VI, Vatican City,

November 18, 1965, section 10, https://www.vatican.va/archive/hist_councils/ii_vatican_council/documents/vat-ii_decree_19651118_apostolicam-actuositatem_en.html.
16 Cited in Daniel P. Horan, "US Bishops Could Learn a Lot from Saint Óscar Romero," *National Catholic Reporter*, February 3, 2021, https://www.ncronline.org/opinion/faith-seeking-understanding/us-bishops-could-learn-lot-st-scar-romero.
17 Julie Hanlon Rubio and Paul J. Schutz, "Beyond 'Bad Apples': Understanding Clergy Perpetrated Sexual Abuse as a Structural Problem and Cultivating Strategies for Change," study, Fordham University, 2022, 1, https://www.scu.edu/media/ignatian-center/bannan/Beyond-Bad-Apples-8-2-FINAL.pdf.
18 Rubio and Schutz, "Beyond 'Bad Apples,'" 16.
19 Rubio and Schutz, "Beyond 'Bad Apples,'" 43.
20 Rubio and Schutz, "Beyond 'Bad Apples,'" 43.
21 Rubio and Schutz, "Beyond 'Bad Apples,'" 40.

CHAPTER FIVE: HUMILITY, COURAGE, AND ALLYSHIP

1 For observant Jews, cleaning the house and specifically the kitchen is a very involved and central part of Passover preparations.
2 J. Mary Luti, "No 'Christian Seders,' Please!," *Sicut Locutus Est: Prayers, Sermons and Marginal Notes* (blog), April 11, 2014, https://sicutlocutusest.com/2014/04/11/no-christian-seders-please.
3 Luti, "No 'Christian Seders.'"
4 Liz Bucar, *Stealing My Religion: Not Just Any Cultural Appropriation* (Cambridge, MA: Harvard University Press, 2022), 207.
5 As Brother David Steindl-Rast reflects, "If we accept and embrace the earthiness of our human condition (and a bit of humor helps) we shall find ourselves doing so with humble pride. In our best moments humility is simply pride that is too grateful to look down on anyone." David Steindl-Rast, *Gratefulness, the Heart of Prayer: An Approach to Life in Fullness* (New York: Paulist, 1984), 203.
6 Dawne Moon and Theresa W. Tobin, "Humility: Rooted in Relationships, Reaching for Justice," *Political Power and Social Theory* 36 (August 5, 2019).
7 Center for Action and Contemplation, "A Clod of Earth," *Daily Meditations*, Center for Action and Contemplation, October 19, 2016, https://cac.org/daily-meditations/a-clod-of-earth-2016-10-19.
8 Karen Armstrong, *Sacred Nature: Restoring Our Ancient Bond with the Natural World* (New York: Alfred A. Knopf, 2022), 70.
9 Stephanie Spellers, *The Church Cracked Open: Disruption, Decline, and a New Hope for Beloved Community* (New York: Church Publishing, 2021), 90.
10 Spellers, *The Church Cracked Open*, 88.

11 Kelly Brown Douglas, "Freedom from Unjust Privilege," *Feminism and Religion* (blog), October 20, 2012, https://feminismandreligion.com/2012/10/20/freedom-from-unjust-privilege-by-kelly-brown-douglas.
12 Henri J.M. Nouwen, *Reaching Out: The Three Movements of the Spiritual Life* (New York: Image, 1975), 89.
13 Pope Francis, *Fratelli Tutti,* Assisi, October 3, 2020, paragraph 116, https://www.vatican.va/content/francesco/en/encyclicals/documents/papa-francesco_20201003_enciclica-fratelli-tutti.html.
14 Hussein Rashid, "Not in the Name of Jesus: On Being True to Ourselves," in *With the Best of Intentions*, ed. Lucinda Mosher, Elinor J. Pierce, and Or N. Rose (Maryknoll, NY: Orbis Books, 2023), 67.
15 Rashid, "Not in the Name," 65.
16 Rashid, "Not in the Name," 65.
17 Joan F. Neal, Robert P. Jones, and Bryan Massingale, "White Supremacy and American Christianity, Part 4: Moving Toward the Beloved Community," event recording, Washington, DC: Network Lobby for Catholic Social Justice, April 6, 2024, https://networklobby.org/actions-to-take-to-after-watching-white-supremacy-in-christianity/.
18 William T. Ditewig, *Courageous Humility: Reflections on the Church, Diakonia, and Deacons* (New York: Paulist, 2022), 240.
19 Harvey Cox, *The Future of Faith* (New York: HarperOne, 2009), 135.
20 Valarie Kaur, *See No Stranger: A Memoir and Manifesto of Revolutionary Love* (New York: OneWorld, 2020), 311.
21 Victoria Atkinson White, *Holy Friendships: Nurturing Relationships That Sustain Pastors and Leaders* (Minneapolis, MN: Fortress Press, 2023), 133.
22 John W. Healey, "From Diversity to Pluralism: The Roman Catholic Challenge and the Roman Catholic Opportunity," in *Education as Transformation: Religious Pluralism, Spirituality, and a New Vision for Higher Education in America*, ed. Victor H. Kazanjian, Jr., and Peter L. Laurence (New York: Peter Lang Verlag, 2021), 125.
23 Adapted from O'Brien, *The Ignatian Adventure*, 75–77.
24 "Being Present," Service Prayers, Xavier University Center for Mission and Identity, accessed May 9, 2024, https://www.xavier.edu/jesuitresource/online-resources/prayer-index/service.

CHAPTER SIX: WELLSPRING OF HOPE: THE SACRAMENT OF INTERFAITH FRIENDSHIP

1 Cited by Carmichael, *Friendship*, 67.
2 John of Taizé, *Friends in Christ*, 86.
3 When I asked my friend Ji Hyang to help me better understand chanting in Buddhism, she directed me to the lens of Soto Zen and a single line in the poem "Song of the Jewel Mirror Samadhi." It reads, "The meaning is not

in the words, yet it responds to the inquiring impulse." The act of reciting in unison brings practitioners together across time and space. This concept of "inquiring impulse" is not unlike beginner's mind.

4   These are actual worries from students, which has prompted a concerted effort to demystify the council and tell the story of this community.
5   Courtney Goto, *The Grace of Playing: Pedagogies for Leaning into God's New Creation* (Eugene, OR: Pickwick, 2016), 3.
6   Goto, 3.
7   Goto, 3.

Bibliography

Aelred of Rievaulx. *Spiritual Friendship*. Edited by Marsha L. Dutton. Translated by Lawrence C. Braceland. Collegeville, MN: Cistercian, 2010.
Armstrong, Karen. *Sacred Nature: Restoring Our Ancient Bond with the Natural World*. New York: Alfred A. Knopf, 2022.
Baldovin, John F., and David Farina Turnbloom. *Catholic Sacraments: A Rich Source of Blessings*. New York: Paulist, 2015.
Barnes, Michael. *Ignatian Spirituality and Interreligious Dialogue: Reading Love's Mystery*. Dublin: Messenger, 2021.
Barry, William A. *A Friendship Like No Other: Experiencing God's Amazing Embrace*. Chicago: Loyola, 2008.
Becker, Karl J., and Ilaria Morali. *Catholic Engagement with World Religions: A Comprehensive Study*. Maryknoll, NY: Orbis Books, 2010.
Boff, Leonardo. *Holy Trinity, Perfect Community*. Translated by Phillip Berryman. Maryknoll, NY: Orbis Books, 2000.
———. *Sacraments of Life: Life of the Sacraments*. Translated by John Drury. Portland, OR: Pastoral Press, 1987.
Bolz-Weber, Nadia. *Day 3 Mass Gathering*. Event recording. Evangelical Lutheran Church in America, June 29, 2018. https://www.youtube.com/watch?v=YBtyZbauH0g.
Boys, Mary C., and Sara S. Lee. *Christians and Jews in Dialogue: Learning in the Presence of the Other*. Woodstock, VT: Skylight Paths, 2006.
Brown, Adrienne Maree. *Emergent Strategy: Shaping Change, Changing Worlds*. Chico, CA: AKPress, 2017.
Bucar, Liz. *Stealing My Religion: Not Just Any Cultural Appropriation*. Cambridge, MA: Harvard University Press, 2022.
Butler, Anthea. *White Evangelical Racism: The Politics of Morality in America*. Chapel Hill: University of North Carolina Press, 2021.
Carmichael, Liz. *Friendship: Interpreting Christian Love*. London: T&T Clark, 2004.
Carr, Nicholas G. *The Shallows: What the Internet Is Doing to Our Brains*. New York: W. W. Norton, 2010.

BIBLIOGRAPHY

Catalano, Roberto. "The Role of Ecclesial Movements in the Implementation of *Nostra Aetate*." In *Catholicism Engaging Other Faiths: Vatican II and its Impact*. Edited by Vladimir Latinovic, Gerard Mannion, and Jason Welle. Part of *Pathways for Ecumenical and Interreligious Dialogue*. Cham, Switzerland: Palgrave Macmillan, 2018. https://doi.org/10.1007/978-3-319-98584-8_6.

Center for Action and Contemplation. "A Clod of Earth." *Daily Meditations*, Center for Action and Contemplation, October 19, 2016. https://cac.org/daily-meditations/a-clod-of-earth-2016-10-19.

Chadwick, Nora. *The Age of the Saints in the Early Celtic Church*. London: Oxford University Press, 1961.

Chittister, Joan. *The Liturgical Year: The Spiraling Adventure of the Spiritual Life*. The Ancient Practices Series. Nashville, TN: Thomas Nelson, 2009.

Cox, Harvey. *The Future of Faith*. New York: HarperOne, 2009.

Ditewig, William T. *Courageous Humility: Reflections on the Church, Diakonia, and Deacons*. New York: Paulist, 2022.

Dubus, Andre. "Sacraments," in *Signatures of Grace: Catholic Writers on the Sacraments*. Edited by Thomas Grady and Paula Huston. Eugene. OR: Wipf and Stock, 2001.

Dulles, Avery. "Vatican II: The Myth and the Reality." *America The Jesuit Review* 188, no. 6 (February 24, 2003). https://www.americamagazine.org/issue/423/article/vatican-ii-myth-and-reality.

Fitzgerald, Michael, and John Borelli. *Interfaith Dialogue: A Catholic View*. Maryknoll, NY: Orbis Books, 2010.

Francis (pope). *Address at the Opening of the Synod of Bishops on Young People, the Faith and Vocational Discernment*. Vatican City, October 3, 2018. https://www.vatican.va/content/francesco/en/speeches/2018/october/documents/papa-francesco_20181003_apertura-sinodo.html.

———. *Evanglii Gaudium*. Vatican City, November 24, 2013. https://www.vatican.va/content/francesco/en/apost_exhortations/documents/papa-francesco_esortazione-ap_20131124_evangelii-gaudium.html.

———. *Fratelli Tutti*. Assisi, October 3, 2020. https://www.vatican.va/content/francesco/en/encyclicals/documents/papa-francesco_20201003_enciclica-fratelli-tutti.html

Franco, Marisa G. *Platonic: How the Science of Attachment Can Help You Make—and Keep—Friends*. New York: Putnam, 2022.

Goshen-Gottstein, Alon. *Friendship across Religions: Theological Perspectives on Interreligious Friendship*. Lanham, MD: Lexington Books, 2015.

Goto, Courtney. *The Grace of Playing: Pedagogies for Leaning into God's New Creation*. Eugene, OR: Pickwick, 2016.

Greeley, Andrew M. *The Catholic Imagination*. Berkeley: University of California Press, 2000.

Harmless, William. *Desert Christians: An Introduction to the Literature of Early Monasticism*. London: Oxford University Press, 2004.

Healey, John W. "From Diversity to Pluralism: The Roman Catholic Challenge and the Roman Catholic Opportunity." In *Education as Transformation: Religious Pluralism, Spirituality, and a New Vision for Higher Education in America*. Edited by Victor H. Kazanjian Jr. and Peter L. Laurence. New York: Peter Lang Verlag, 2021.

Heyward, Carter. *Saving Jesus from Those Who Are Right: Rethinking What It Means to Be Christian*. Minneapolis, MN: Fortress Press, 1999.

Hilkert, Mary Catherine. *Naming Grace: Preaching and the Sacramental Imagination*. New York: Continuum, 2006.

Himes, Michael. *The Mystery of Faith: An Introduction to Catholicism*. Cincinnati, OH: Franciscan Media, 2004.

Horan, Daniel P. "US Bishops Could Learn a Lot from Saint Óscar Romero." *National Catholic Reporter*, February 3, 2021. https://www.ncronline.org/opinion/faith-seeking-understanding/us-bishops-could-learn-lot-st-scar-romero.

Hughes, Kathleen. *Becoming the Sign: Sacramental Living in a Post-Conciliar Church*. New York: Paulist, 2013.

Hunt, Mary. *Fierce Tenderness: A Feminist Theology of Friendship*. Chestnut Ridge, NY: Crossroad, 1992.

John of Taizé. *Friends in Christ: Paths to a New Understanding of Church*. Maryknoll, NY: Orbis Books, 2012.

Johnson, Elizabeth A. *She Who Is: The Mystery of God in Feminist Theological Discourse*. Chestnut Ridge, NY: Crossroad, 1992.

Johnson, Nathan C. "When Seventy Equals Seventy-Two: A Reception-Historical Contribution to the Text-Critical Problem of Luke 10:1, 17." *Journal of Theological Studies* 70, no. 2 (July 2019): 650. https://doi.org/10.1093/jts/flz084.

Jones, Robert P., Bryan Massingale, and Marcia Chatelain. *White Supremacy and American Christianity*. Event recording. Washington, DC: Network Lobby for Catholic Social Justice, April 9, 2022. https://networklobby.org/uschristianityconvo/.

Kaur, Valarie. *See No Stranger: A Memoir and Manifesto of Revolutionary Love*. New York: One World, 2020.

Konieczny, Mary Ellen, Charles C. Camosy, and Tricia C. Bruce. *Polarization in the US Catholic Church: Naming the Wounds, Beginning to Heal*. Collegeville, MN: Liturgical Press, 2016.

LaCugna, Catherine Mowry. *God for Us: The Trinity and Christian Life*. San Francisco: HarperCollins, 1991.

———. "The Practical Trinity." *The Christian Century* 109 no. 2 (July 15–22, 1992).

Largen, Kristin Johnston, Mary E. Hess, and Christy Lohr Sapp. *Interreligious Learning and Teaching: A Christian Rationale for a Transformative Praxis*. Minneapolis, MN: Fortress Press, 2014.

Larson, Marion H., and Sarah L. H. Shady. *From Bubble to Bridge: Educating Christians for a Multifaith World*. Downer's Grove, IL: InterVarsity, 2017.

Latinovic, Vladimir, Gerard Mannion, and Jason Welle. *Catholicism Engaging Other Faiths: Vatican II and its Impact*. Cham, Switzerland: Palgrave McMillan, 2018.

Leonardo, Nixaly. *Active Listening Techniques: 20 Practical Tools to Hone your Communication Skills*. Emeryville, CA: Rockridge, 2020.

Luciani, Rafael. *Synodality: A New Way of Proceeding in the Church*. New York: Paulist, 2022.

Mannion, G. "Catholicism Embracing Its Religious Others." In *Catholicism Engaging Other Faiths: Vatican II and its Impact*. Edited by Vladimir Latinovic, Gerard Mannion, and Jason Welle. Part of *Pathways for Ecumenical and Interreligious Dialogue*. Cham, Switzerland: Palgrave Macmillan, 2018. https://doi.org/10.1007/978-3-319-98584-8_1.

Martos, Joseph. *Doors to the Sacred: A Historical Introduction to Sacraments in the Catholic Church*. Ligouri, MO: Ligouri, 2014.

Massingale, Bryan N. *Racial Justice and the Catholic Church*. Maryknoll, NY: Orbis Books, 2010.

McColman, Carl. *The Big Book of Christian Mysticism: The Essential Guide to Contemplative Spirituality*. San Francisco: Hampton Roads, 2010.

———. *Befriending Silence: Discovering the Gifts of Cistercian Spirituality*. Notre Dame, IN: Ave Maria, 2015.

Merton, Thomas. *New Seeds of Contemplation*. New York: New Directions, 2007.

———. *Thoughts in Solitude*. New York: Farrar, Straus & Giroux, 1958.

Moon, Dawne, and Theresa W. Tobin. "Humility: Rooted in Relationships, Reaching for Justice." *Political Power and Social Theory* 36 (August 5, 2019).

Moore, Mary Elizabeth Mullino. *Teaching as a Sacramental Act*. Cleveland, OH: Pilgrim, 2004.

Neal, Joan F., Robert P. Jones, and Bryan Massingale. *White Supremacy and American Christianity, Part 4: Moving Toward the Beloved Community*. Event recording. Washington, DC: Network Lobby for Catholic Social Justice, April 6, 2024. https://networklobby.org/actions-to-take-to-after-watching-white-supremacy-in-christianity/.

Nouwen, Henri J. M. *Reaching Out: The Three Movements of the Spiritual Life*. New York: Image, 1975.

O'Brien, Kevin. *The Ignatian Adventure: Experiencing the Spiritual Exercises of Saint Ignatius in Daily Life*. Chicago: Loyola, 2011.

O'Donohue, John. *Anam Cara: A Book of Celtic Wisdom*. New York: HarperCollins, 1997.

Ospino, Hosffman. *No Synodal Church Without Catechetical Reform*. Lecture. Brighton, MA: Gloria L. and Charles I. Clough School of Theology and Ministry, Boston College, October 12, 2023. https://www.bc.edu/content/bc-web/schools/stm/sites/encore/main/2023/no-synodal-church-without-catechetical-reform.html.

Padma, JiHyang. *Living the Season: Zen Practices for Transformative Times.* Wheaton, IL: Quest Books, 2013.

Paintner, Christine Valters. "The Desert Mothers and Fathers Showed Us All Life is Sacred: Experience God in Every Moment." *US Catholic* 85, no. 2 (January 31, 2020): 20–23. https://uscatholic.org/articles/202001/discover-the-sacredness-of-life-with-the-desert-mothers-and-fathers.

Pawlikowski, J. T. "Nostra Aetate: Where It Has Taken Us; Where We Still Need to Go." In *Catholicism Engaging Other Faiths: Vatican II and Its Impact.* Edited by Vladimir Latinovic, Gerard Mannion, and Jason Welle. Part of *Pathways for Ecumenical and Interreligious Dialogue.* Cham, Switzerland: Palgrave Macmillan, 2018. https://doi.org/10.1007/978-3-319-98584-8_5.

Patel, Eboo, Jennifer Howe Peace, and Noah J. Silverman, eds. *Interreligious/Interfaith Studies: Defining a New Field.* Boston: Beacon, 2018.

Peace, Jennifer Howe, Or N. Rose, and Gregory Mobley, eds. *My Neighbor's Faith: Stories of Interreligious Encounter, Growth, and Transformation.* Maryknoll, NY: Orbis Books, 2012.

Pontifical Council for Inter-Religious Dialogue. *Dialogue and Proclamation.* Vatican City, May 19, 1991. https://www.vatican.va/roman_curia/pontifical_councils/interelg/documents/rc_pc_interelg_doc_19051991_dialogue-and-proclamatio_en.html.

Rambachan, Anantanand. "'Love Speaking to Love:' Friendship Across Religious Traditions." In *Friendship Across Religions: Theological Perspectives on Interreligious Friendship.* Edited by Alon Goshen-Gottstein. New York: Lexington Books, 2015.

Rashid, Hussein. "Not in the Name of Jesus: On Being True to Ourselves." In *With the Best of Intentions.* Edited by Lucinda Mosher, Elinor J. Pierce, and Or N. Rose. Maryknoll, NY: Orbis Books, 2023.

Rogers, Carl R., and Richard E. Farson. *Active Listening.* Mansfield Centre, CT: Martino, 2015.

Rohr, Richard. *The Divine Dance: The Trinity and Your Transformation.* New Kensington, PA: Whitaker House, 2016.

Ross, Susan. *Extravagant Affections: A Feminist Sacramental Theology.* New York: Continuum, 2001.

Rubio, Julie Hanlon, and Paul J. Schutz. "Beyond 'Bad Apples': Understanding Clergy Perpetrated Sexual Abuse as a Structural Problem and Cultivating Strategies for Change." Study, Fordham University, 2022. https://www.scu.edu/media/ignatian-center/bannan/Beyond-Bad-Apples-8-2-FINAL.pdf.

Russell, Letty M. *Just Hospitality: God's Welcome in a World of Difference.* Edited by J. Shannon Clarkson and Kate M. Ott. Louisville, KY: Westminster John Knox, 2009.

Secretariat for Non-Christians. *The Attitude of the Church Toward the Followers of Other Religions: Reflections and Orientations on Dialogue and Mission.* Address of the Pope. Vatican City, March 3, 1984. https://www.

dicasteryinterreligious.va/wp-content/uploads/2021/06/Dialogue_and_Mission_ENG.pdf.

———. *The Attitude of the Church Toward Followers of Other Religions: Reflections on Dialogue and Mission*. Vatican City, May 10, 1984. https://www.cam1.org.au/Portals/66/documents/Dialogue-Mission-1984.pdf.

Segura, Olga M. *Birth of a Movement: Black Lives Matter and the Catholic Church*. Maryknoll, NY: Orbis Books, 2021.

Sellner, Edward C. *Stories of Celtic Soul Friends: Their Meaning for Today*. New York: Paulist, 2004.

Simpson, Ray. *Soul Friendship in the Celtic Tradition: Ancient Insights for Today*. Vestal, NY: Anamchara Books, 2021.

Spellers, Stephanie. *The Church Cracked Open: Disruption, Decline, and New Hope for Beloved Community*. New York: Church Publishing, 2021.

Steindl-Rast, David. *Gratefulness, the Heart of Prayer: An Approach to Life in Fullness*. New York: Paulist, 1984.

Suzuki, Shunryu. *Zen Mind, Beginner's Mind: Informal Talks on Zen Meditation and Practice*. New York: Weatherhill, 1980.

Swan, Laura. *The Forgotten Desert Mothers: Sayings, Lives, and Stories of Early Christian Women*. New York: Paulist, 2001.

Tertullian, "De Corona Militis." Translated by S. Thelwell. From *Ante-Nicene Fathers* vol. 3, *Tertullian*. Edited by Alexander Roberts, James Donaldson, and A. Cleveland Coxe. Revised and edited for *New Advent* by Kevin Knight. Buffalo, NY: Christian Literature Publishing, 1885. http://www.newadvent.org/fathers/0304.htm.

Thích Nhất Hạnh. *The Art of Communicating*. New York: HarperOne, 2013.

———. *The Art of Living*. New York: HarperOne, 2017.

Turkle, Sherry. *Reclaiming Conversation: The Power of Talk in a Digital Age*. New York: Penguin, 2015.

Vatican Council II. *Declaration on the Relation of the Church to Non-Christian Religions:* Nostra Aetate. Promulgated by Pope Paul VI. Vatican City, October 28, 1965. https://www.vatican.va/archive/hist_councils/ii_vatican_council/documents/vat-ii_decl_19651028_nostra-aetate_en.html.

———. *Decree on the Apostolate of the Laity: Apostolicam Actuositatem*. Promulgated by Pope Paul VI. Vatican City, November 18, 1965. https://www.vatican.va/archive/hist_councils/ii_vatican_council/documents/vat-ii_decree_19651118_apostolicam-actuositatem_en.html.

———. *Dogmatic Constitution on the Church: Lumen Gentium*. Promulgated by Pope Paul VI. Vatican City, November 21, 1964. https://www.vatican.va/archive/hist_councils/ii_vatican_council/documents/vat-ii_const_19641121_lumen-gentium_en.html.

Vento, Johann M. "The Sacramentality of Inter-Religious Friendship." Jerusalem: The Elijah Interfaith Institute, November 4, 2015. https://elijah-interfaith.org/sharing-wisdom/the-sacramentality-of-inter-religious-friendship.

Volf, Miroslav, and Ryan McAnnally-Linz. "A Christian Perspective on Interreligious Friendship." Jerusalem: The Elijah Interfaith Institute, November 4, 2015. https://elijah-interfaith.org/sharing-wisdom/a-christian-perspective-on-interreligious-friendship.

Wadell, Paul J. *Becoming Friends: Worship, Justice, and the Practice of Christian Friendship.* Grand Rapids, MI: Brazos, 2002.

White, Victoria Atkinson. *Holy Friendships: Nurturing Relationships that Sustain Pastors and Leaders.* Minneapolis, MN: Fortress Press, 2023.

Zagano, Phyllis. *Just Church: Catholic Social Teaching, Synodality, and Women.* New York: Paulist, 2023.

Further Reading

Included in this short list are books that I have found to be particularly formative in my own thinking and prayer life. I consider several of these texts to be good friends, resources I go back to time and again. It is not meant to be an exhaustive list but just another entry point.

Boff, Leonardo. *Sacraments of Life: Life of the Sacraments.* Translated by John Drury. Portland, OR: Pastoral Press, 1987.
His Holiness the Dalai Lama, Archbishop Desmond Tutu, and Douglas Abrams. *The Book of Joy: Lasting Happiness in a Changing World.* New York: Random House, 2016.
Horan, Daniel P. *A White Catholic's Guide to Racism and Privilege.* Notre Dame, IN: Ave Maria Press, 2021.
Jean-Charles, Régine. *Martin Luther King and the Trumpet of Conscience Today.* Maryknoll, NY: Orbis Press, 2021.
Knitter, Paul. *One Earth Many Religions: Multifaith Dialogue and Global Responsibility.* Maryknoll, NY: Orbis Press, 1995.
Knitter, Paul. *Without Buddha I Could Not Be a Christian.* London: OneWorld Academic, 2013.
Lindahl, Kay. *Practicing the Sacred Art of Listening: A Guide to Enrich Your Relationships and Kindle Your Spiritual Life.* Woodstock, VT: Skylight Paths Publishing, 2012.
Matlins, Stuart M. *How to Be a Perfect Stranger: The Essential Religious Etiquette Handbook.* 6th ed. Woodstock, VT: Skylight Paths Publishing, 2015.
Mosher, Lucinda, Elinor J. Pierce, and Or N. Rose, eds. *With the Best of Intentions: Interreligious Missteps and Mistakes.* Maryknoll, NY: Orbis Press, 2023.
Peace, Jennifer Howe, Or N. Rose, and Gregory Mobley, eds. *My Neighbor's Faith: Stories of Interreligious Encounter, Growth, and Transformation.* Maryknoll, NY: Orbis Books, 2012.
Taylor, Barbara Brown. *Holy Envy: Finding God in the Faith of Others.* New York: HarperOne, 2019.
Thích Nhất Hạnh. *The Art of Communicating.* New York: HarperOne, 2013.

Index

Abba/Amma/Seeker relationships, anamcara and, 25
accessibility, spirit of, 54–55
actions, of people, 42
active listening
    Carl Rogers and, 77–79
    central component of, 78
    cultivating and refining muscles for, 145
    mono-tasking and, 83
    practicing, 79–80
    skills, 88
Acts of the Apostles, 71
Age of the Saints in Early Celtic Church, The (Chadwick), 25
allyship, 143
Anamcara. *See* Soul friend
Anam Cara: A Book of Celtic Wisdom (O'Donohue), 12
Ambrose, Saint, 30
Angell, Heather, 34, 45, 49, 64, 135, 136
anti-Catholicism, 135–36
anticlericalism and equipping the saints, 119–22
Apostolicam Acousitatem, 109

art, use of, 75
artwork, praying with, 75
Atkinson, Victoria White, 145
Attitude of the Church toward Followers of Other Religious: Reflections and Orientations on Dialogue and Mission, The, 59
authenticity, 127, 138
    of people, 57
    spirit of, 54–55
    vulnerability and, 32, 34

Baldovin, John F., 95, 98, 100, 117
baptized
    Archbishop Romero dream for, 118
    gift of being, 109–10
    LaCugna empowering the, 54
    Vatican II documents and, 109
Barry, William A., 33, 35
Becoming the Sign: Sacramental Living in a Post-Concilar Church (Hughes), 101
Befriending Silence (McColman), 84
Beyond 'Bad Apples': "Understanding Clergy Perpetrated Sexual

INDEX

Abuse as a Structural Problem and Cultivating Strategies for Change", 120
Big Book of Christian Mysticism (McColman), 83
Black activists, 143
Black Lives Matter, 143
blessing oneself, practice of, 50
Boff, Leonardo, 46, 47, 102, 104, 107
Bolz-Weber, Nadia, 110
Brigid of Kildare, Saint, 26–27, 81
Bucar, Liz, 128, 129
Buddhist chaplain, 67, 152, 153

Cain and Abel, rivalry between, 141
Cambridge Zen Center, 152–53
caring for others, 33
carnal friendship, 31
Cassian, John, 22
Catalano, Roberto, 60
Catholic Church
    American, 141
    documents defining relationships in, 58–64
    use of the term interreligious in, 8
Catholic community
    alums roles in, 110–11
    Julie and, 4
    Mandy as president of, 156–57
    May a student from, 125–28, 129, 130
    students on importance of, 3
"Catholic imaginative", Greeley on, 104
Catholic peace movement, 45
Catholics
    approach to interfaith work, 130
    courage as gift of the Holy Spirit, 139
    living a life as, 95–96
    Nostra Aetate (NA) impact on, 59
    See also Catholic Church; Catholic community
Catholic Social Teaching (CST), 58, 135
Celtic Church tradition, 24, 25
Celtic festival of Imbolc, 26
Chadwick, Nora, 25
chaplaincy
    check-in with, 86
    humanist, 111, 113
    introducing students to diverse practices and, 104
    listening to Catholic students and, 3
    prayer to guide in lifelong work, 149
    student and Lenten practices, 101
    transformation, conversion, and connection in, 146
    See also higher education chaplaincy; multifaith chaplaincy; university chaplaincy
cheap solidarity, 140
Chittister, Sister Joan, 63
Christ
    caring for, 33
    love of friends and love of, 32
Christianity
    friendship as central theme in, 12
    Jesus and, 88
    spread of, 25–26
Christian life
    dialogue and mission and, 62

INDEX

religious, concept of soul friend in, 21
spiritual friendship as necessity in, 30
Christian monastics, 22
Christian privilege and white Christian nationalism, 136–39
Christian(s)
in dialogue, 64
friendship, Aelred of Rievaulx on, 30
reality of Holy Trinity and, 38
Seders, 125, 126–27
tradition, 22–23
See also Christianity; desert Christians
Christian spirituality, 25–26
Christian supremacy, white Christian supremacy and, 134
Chrysostom, Saint John, 12
Church
attracting people to, 133
clericalism and, 114–16
humanity and, 61
relationship to other religious traditions, 61
teaching, human experience and, 48
in the twenty-first century, 74
See also Catholic church
Church Cracked Open, The (Spellers), 134
clericalism, 111, 113
addressing sickness within church, 116–19
as defined by Rubio and Schutz, 120
unlearning the clericalism within, 119–22
client-centered approach, 77
College of Bishops, 74
Common Era, soul friend in, 21
common exploration, 64
conciliar documents, 58–64
connection, joy of, 16
contemplation, as component of Lectio Divina, 124
conversion in DM, 90–92
Corinthians 12:27-31, 123–24
Council of Nicaea, 48
courage, role of, 139–40
Covid-19 pandemic, 98, 153
challenge of, 66
community mid/post-pandemic, 66–67
first summer at the beach during, 106–7
formation of working group at beginning of, 86
impact on religious imaginations, 98–99
loneliness and, 12, 28, 107
sacramental consciousness and, 98–99
worship after, 65–67
Cox, Harvey, 141
CST. *See* Catholic Social Teaching (CST)

Dance of Trinity, 52–53
Declaration on the Relation of the Church to Non-Christian Religions: The, Nostra Aetate, The (In our Time):, 57–58, 59–60, 61–62, 134

INDEX

Decree of the Apostolate of the Laity, 117, 119
desert Christians, 24, 26
   religious imaginations and, 22
   solitude, friendship and, 23
desert elders, as spiritual mentors or soul friends, 23
Desert Mothers and Fathers, 21–23, 30, 122
desert stories, on soul friend, 21–22
dharma talk, 163
Dialogue and Mission (DM)
   Christian life and, 62
   conversion in, 90–92
   interfaith dialogue and, 62
   powerful elements of, 62–63
Dialogue and Mission (DM), 58
Dialogue and Proclamation: Reflection and Orientations on Interreligious Dialogue and Proclamation of the Gospel of Jesus Christ, 1994, 58
Dialogue of Action, 62, 63
Dialogue of Experience (or Theological Exchange), 62
Dialogue of Life, 62–63
Dialogue of Religious Experience, 62, 63, 64–67
Dialogue of Theological Exchange, 63
Dignitas Humanae (Declaration of Religious Freedom), 1965, 59, 62
discipleship, ownership and missionary, 109–13
discourse, role in interfaith work, 138
distractions
   experiencing, 81
   O'Brien on, 82
Ditewig, William, 140
Divine Dance, The (Rohr), 50
divinity school, interfaith gathering at, 137–38
(DM 3), 62
(DM 7), 62
DM 29, 30, 63
Doctrine of Trinity
   bringing into our lives, 55
   concept of, 54–55
   LaCugna on, 53–54, 55
   reality of Trinity and, 47–48
documents, conciliar and postconciliar, 58–64
Douglas, Kelly Brown, 135
Dubus, Andre, 105, 106

Emmaus, walk of, 21
"emotional entanglements", 30
empathy
   building, 7
   client-centered approach and, 77
   working to increase, 5
enchanted imagination, Greeley on, 104
enchantment, dwelling in, 106–9
Eucharist, Liturgy of, 109
evangelization, 7, 110
Evangeli Gaudium (apostolic exhortation), 110
Examen
   experimenting with, 148
   in spiritual life, 146–47
   ways to pray the, 147–48

INDEX

faith, the word, 8
Farson, Richard, 77
feedback, in practicing active listening, 80
Floyd, George, 143
forgiveness, rejoicing and seeking, 147
Fort Benning, Georgia, 45
friend(s)
    of God, 33–39
    love of Christ and love of, 32
    Paul on, 31
    spiritual, spiritual life and, 13
    See also Friendship(s); Soul friend
Friendship Blessing, A (O'Donohue), 27–28
friendship in the tradition, 11–43
    Aelred of Rievaulx's spiritual friendship, 30–33
    anamcara, 26–28
    desert of loneliness, 28–29
    friends of God, 33–37
    friendship in scripture, 13–16
    gift of being seen, 40–42
    the seventy-two, 17–21
    soul friend, 21–26
    spiritual provocation, 17, 39–40, 42–43
    we are God's friends too, 37–39
Friendship Like No Other: Experiencing God's Amazing Embrace, A (Barry), 33
friendship(s)
    Abba and Amma, 22, 23, 24
    according to Brother John of Taizé, 37
    advantages of, 32
    bond of, 11–12
    interfaith, 144
    intra-faith, 141–42
    of Jesus, Mary, Martha, and Lazarus, 13–14
    kinds of, 31
    McEvoy on, 161–62
    in monastic communities, 30–31
    role in spiritual life, 41
    in scripture, 13–17
    words of Jesus and, 17
    See also Spiritual friendship program
Friends in Christ: Paths to a New Understanding of Church (Brother John of Taizé), 34
Future of Faith, The (Cox), 141

Gaillardetz, Richard, 99–100
Gaudium et Spes (Pastoral Constitution on the Church in the Modern World, 1965), 59, 61
gift
    of being seen, 40–42
    of humility, 131–33
    of revelation, 55–57
God
    asking for guidance, 148
    friends of, 33–37
    imaging and experiencing, 39–40
    listening to, 80–83
    magnitude of love, 43
    McColman on greatness of, 82–83
    praying for help and thanking, 147
    relationship with, 83

INDEX

relationship with one another
and, 54–55
as Trinity, 53
triune, 48, 49
turning toward and away from,
147
Goddard Chapel, 65, 84
God for Us (LaCugna), 53
Goto, Courtney, 167–69
Grace of Play, The (Goto), 167
gracious self-gift, 64
gratitude, humility and, 132
Greater Boston Interfaith
Organization, 115
Greeley, Andrew, 104
Gregory of Nazianzus, 52

Hanh, Thích Nhất (Vietnamese
teacher and leader), 67–68
Healey, John, 146
heartifact (term), 158
Heschel, Rabbi Abraham Joshua, 5
Heyward, Carter, 53
higher education, loneliness and,
17–18
higher education chaplaincy, 95–96,
119–20
Holly (chaplain), 82, 152
holy, in the everyday, 96–109
*Holy Friendships: Nurturing
Relationships That Sustain
Pastors and Leaders*
(Atkinson), 145
Holy Spirit, 8, 32, 151
courage as gift of, 139
guidance, 147, 151, 170–71
listening to, 74

moment, 5, 6, 103
Holy Trinity
in context of, 46–48
intersections and interdependence,
46
theopoetic, 48–51
hospitality, forms of, 154–56
Hughes, Kathleen, 101
human, meaning of, 133–34
human experience, church teaching
and, 48
human family, 60
Humanism, 111, 112
humanity, church and, 61
humility, courage, and allyship,
125–49
Christian privilege and white
Christian nationalism,
136–39
gift of humility, 131–33
intra-faith friendships, 141–42
joy of preparation, 144–46
kenosis, or self-emptying,
133–35
power of small connections–the
Examen, 146–49
role of courage, 139–40
showing up and sticking around,
143–44
Hunt, Mary, 104–5, 106, 161
Hyang, Ji, 7

Ignatian Adventure (O'Brien), 82
Ignatian Contemplation, 37
Ignatian Spirituality, 148
Imaginative Prayer or Composition
of Place, 37

independence and difference, 45–68
  dance of trinity, 52–53
  holy trinity in context, 46–48
  relationality, 54–68
  signpost trinity, 53–54
  theopoetic of the holy trinity, 48–51
interactions, importance of, 146
Interfaith Center, 5, 56, 153, 160
interfaith dialogue, 57, 59, 62
interfaith engagement, 7, 74, 114, 120, 144, 151, 169
interfaith family, 125
interfaith friendship, 96, 144, 152, 164, 169
interfaith friendship, sacrament of, 151–71
interfaith friendship program, 19, 67
interfaith gathering, 137–38, 148
Interfaith Student Council (ISC), 4, 92, 157–60, 164
interfaith work, 112, 122, 130
  disputes, disagreements, and, 141
  engaging in, 137
  experience in, 3, 46
  positionality and identity and, 130
  role of kenotic humility in, 147
  role of power and discourse in, 138
  transformative, 169
interreligious dialogue, 63–64
interreligious/interfaith studies, 8
intra-faith friendships, 141–42
ISC. *See Interfaith Student Council (ISC)*

Jamie's story, 114–16
Jesus
  asking the disciples to fish, 38
  commissioning the seventy-two, 21
  framing the heart of his teaching, 16
  Kenosis and, 134–35
  Mary, Martha, and Lazarus, 13–17
  self-emptying as referred by Paul's letter, 133
  teaching true discipleship, 19–20
  words of, 17
Jewish friends, sharing holy space with, 65–67
John, Gospel of, 14, 37
John of Taizé, Brother, 34–35, 36, 37, 162
Johnson, Elizabeth, 48
Julie's story, 4–6

Kaur, Valarie (Sikh activist), 142
Kendi, Ibram X., 120
kenosis, or self-emptying, 133–35
King, Martin Luther Jr., 5

LaCugna
  on adoration, 57
  Catherine Mowry, 52, 53–54, 55
laity, power of, 114–16
layfolk
  clergy and, 117–18
  clericalism and, 116
Lectio Divina (divine reading), 74–75, 122
Lenten simple supper, 56

INDEX

lifelong work, 87–88
limits, knowing one's, 162–64
listening
   contagious, 77
   creating a container, 86
   silence and, 84
   transformative act of, 160–62
   See also Active listening
listening to God, ourselves and one another, 69–93
   active listening practice, 79–80
   conversion in DM, 90–92
   creating a container to listen, 86–87
   lifelong work, 87–88
   listening and transformation, 69
   listening church, 73–75
   listening in scripture with Lydia, 70–73
   listening to the music of our lives, 92–93
   listening to the world around us, 80–83
   mindfulness, 84–85
   mono-tasking, 83–84
   Nancy's conversion, 88–90, 145
   what happens when we listen, 75–79
loneliness, 105
   after loss, 143
   cost of, 161
   Covid-19 pandemic and, 12, 28, 107
   culture and, 162
   desert of, 28–29
   vulnerability problem and, 17–18
   See also solitude

loss
   of dear friend, 40
   time of profound, 37–38
love, joy with, 16
Luke, Gospel of, 14, 19
Lumen Gentium, 109
Luti, Mary, 126
Lydia, listening in scripture with, 70–73

Mary/Maryam program, 161–62
Massingale, Fr. Bryan, 139, 140
Matthew, Gospel of, 33, 88
McColman, Carl, 82–83
McEvoy, James, 161–62
meditation
   as component of Lectio Divina, 122
   mindfulness, 85
Merton, Thomas, 36
mindfulness, 84–85
monastic communities, friendship in, 30–31
monastic spirituality, 25
mono-tasking, 83–84
moral courage, 140
multifaith, 8
multifaith chaplaincy, 45–68, 164
Multitasking, 83, 84–85
Muslim chaplain (Celene), 154–56
mutual relation, 53
mutual witness, 64

Nancy's conversion, 88–91, 145
"New attitude" phrase, Catalano and, 60
New Testament, Jesus and his friends, the disciples in, 12

non-Christian, phrase of, 8
nonverbal connection, active listening and, 78
Nostra Aetate (document), 57–58, 59–60, 61–62, 134
"Not in the Name of Jesus: On Being True to Ourselves" (Rashid), 138
Nouwen, Henri, 135

O'Brien, Kevin, 82
O'Donohue John, 12, 27
openness to self-redefinition, 146

painter, Benedictine Oblate Christine Valters, 24–25
pan-religious, 8
Passover Seder tradition, 125, 126, 127, 129
patience, value of, 170
Paul
    about friends carrying each other's burdens, 31
    finding place of prayer, 73
    letter to the Ephesians, 119
    letter to the Philippians, 133
    Lydia listening to, 71, 72
perichoresis
    challenges of, 53
    defined, 52
Person *(hypostasis)*, as defined by Boff, 46
personal spiritual reflection, trinitarian theology and, 45–68
perversion, meaning of, 117
Pope Francis, 117, 118
    Evangeli Gaudium, 110
    solidarity in the words of, 135

vision of journeying together, 73–74
postconciliar documents, 58–64
power, in interfaith work, 138
prayer/praying
    as component of Lectio Divina, 123–24
    for God's help, 147
    spiritual life and connection to, 36–37
preparation, joy of, 144–46
Priya (Buddhist Chaplain), 67
Proclamation and Dialogue, 63
proselytization
    interfaith engagement and, 7
    mission work and, 62
psalm, 42, 43, 104

racism and anti-racism, 120
Radical Amazement, 5–6, 12
"Raising of Lazarus", 14
Rambachan, Anantanand, 7
Rashid, Hussein, 138–39
reading, as component of Lectio Divina, 123
reflecting back, 79
reflection, active listening and, 79
relationality, 54–68
relationship(s)
    building new, 29
    call to be in, 57–58
    documents defining Catholic Church about, 58–64
    in trinitarian theology, 54–55
religion, love with the study of, 2–3
"religious appropriation", Bucar on, 128
religious commitment, 64

religious education, 100
religious literacy, 144–45, 160–62
religious minorities, 4, 7, 128, 137
religious other, phrase of, 8
revelation, gift of, 55–57
revelatory experiencing, 164–71
Rievaulx, Alfred of, 30–33, 40
Rogers, Carl, 77–79
Rohr, Richard, 50–51, 62, 100–101, 132–33, 171
Romero, Õscar (Archbishop), 118
Rubio, Julie Hanlon, 120–21
Russell, Letty, 154

"Sacrament" (Dubus), 105
sacramental consciousness, expanding, 95–96, 102–6
sacramental consciousness and participation, 95–124
   the holy in everyday, 96–109
   ownership and missionary discipleship, 109–19
   spiritual practice, 122–24
   unlearning the clericalism within, 119–22
sacramental imagination, Hunt on, 104–5
sacramental living, 101
sacramental rite, 101
sacrament(s)
   Boff about, 103
   of the church, 107
   defined, 100–101
Sacraments of Life and a Life of Sacraments, The (Boff), 102–3
sacred calendaring, 165, 167
Sacrosanctum Concilium, 109

Saint Ignatius's Composition of Place, 42
Santa Clara University, clericalism study, 120
SBNR. *See* Spiritual But Not Religious)
School of the Americas, 45
Schutz, Paul, 120–21
scripture
   friendship in, 13–17
   listening in scripture with Lydia, 70–73
Seekers
   desert elders as soul friends to, 23
   discernment process of, 23–24
"Self-disclosure" as strength to relationships, 23
Sellner, Edward, 26
Seven Sacraments, 100, 117
Shabbat service, 65–67
shared spiritual practice model, 18
showing up and sticking around, 143–44
Signpost trinity, 53–54
silence
   active listening and, 78–79
   attentiveness to, 81
   listening and, 84
Simon Peter, going out fishing, 37–39
Simpson, Ray, 27
sincerity, 64
Solidarity, Principle of, 135
solitude, connection and, 23
soul friend(s), 12
   desert elders as spiritual mentors or, 23
   Desert Mothers and Fathers, 21–23

as gift, 26–28
practical conversation of, 28
role of, 133–35
Saint Brigid and, 27
spiritual life and, 21
See also Angell, Heather
Soul Friendship in the Celtic Tradition: Ancient Insights for Today (Simpson), 27
Spellers, Stephanie, 134
spirit
of accessibility and authenticity, 54–55
of *Nostra Aetate* in real life, 61–62
'Spirit of truth', 74
Spiritual But Not Religious (SBNR), 139
spiritual care, 86–87
spiritual companionship, 21–22
spiritual friend, 13, 32
Spiritual Friendship (Aelred of Rievaulx), 30–33, 40
spiritual friendship program, 17–21
evolving into interfaith friendship program, 19
invitation to the community to participate, 18–19
origin of, 17–18
practicing what was preached, 19
the seventy-two, 19–21
spirituality, Christian, 25–26, 82
spiritual life, 13
about, 36–37, 101
concept of soul friend in, 21
Examen in, 146–47
experience and shaping, 2
friendship and, 12

Holly about, 152
Jamie's interfaith engagement and, 114–16
religious/philosophical traditions and, 6
role of friendship in, 41
spiritual friend and, 13
spiritual practice, 82, 84–85, 122–24
spiritual provocation
bearing fruit, 17
God Understands you, 42–43
holy urgency, 39
interbeing, 67–68
listening to the Music to our Lives, 92–93
Power of Small Connections, the Examen, 146–49
sites of meeting, 51
Stations of Holy Water, 48
Stealing My Religion (Bucar), 128
story slam
in Boston, 5, 75–76
in Jamaica Plain, 69
storytelling and story receiving, 79
Suzuki, Shunryu, 87–88
Synodality: The listening church, 73–75

tension, preparedness for, 171
terminology, 8
Tertullian (third century church father), 50
"The mind of Christ", phrase, 61
the seventy-two, 17–21
transformation, condition of, 77

INDEX

transgender student, Sister Nancy and, 88–90
Trinitarian interdependence, 48
Trinitarian living, movement as essence of, 53
Trinitarian theology, 45–68
  multifaith chaplaincy and, 46
Trinity
  dance of, 52–53
  as defined by Rohr, 51
  doctrine of, 47–48, 54–55
  God as, 53
  Heyward reflection on, 53
  interdependence and, 46
  meaning of, 48
  as mystery, 50–51
  signpost, 53–54
triune God, 48, 49
trust
  building, client-centered approach and, 77
  O'Brien and, 82
Tufts Buddhist mindfulness sangha, 152
Tufts Hillel, 65, 66, 129, 153, 165
Tufts University, 8, 17–21, 67, 160, 164
Turkle, Sherry, 83

UCC. *See* United Church of Christ
Uni, Father Jon, 132
United Church of Christ (UCC), 126
University Chaplaincy, 65, 86, 114

Vatican II documents, 109
Visio Divina (divine seeing/gazing), 74

wellspring of hope (the sacrament of interfaith friendship), 151–71
  creating a container, 156–60
  forms of hospitality, 154–56
  getting comfortable being uncomfortable, 152–54
  knowing one's limits, 162–64
  religious literacy, 160–62
  revelatory experiencing, 164–71
white Christian nationalism, 140
white Christian Supremacy, 134
world around us, listening to the, 80–83
worldly friendship, 31

zafu (meditation cushion), 152
Zen Buddhism, 87
Zen Mind (Suzuki), 88

www.ingramcontent.com/pod-product-compliance
Ingram Content Group UK Ltd.
Pitfield, Milton Keynes, MK11 3LW, UK
UKHW030435270625
460145UK00002B/168